the advent lyrics
of the
exeter book

# the advent lyrics of the exeter book

EDITED, WITH INTRODUCTION AND NOTES

BY JACKSON J. CAMPBELL

PRINCETON, NEW JERSEY

PRINCETON UNIVERSITY PRESS

1959

Copyright © 1959 by Princeton University Press
All Rights Reserved
The Library of Congress catalog entry for this book appears at end of text

Publication of this book has been aided by the
Ford Foundation program
to support publication, through university presses,
of works in the humanities and social sciences,
and also by the
John E. Annan Memorial Fund
and by the Research Fund
of Princeton University.

Printed in the United States of America by
Princeton University Press, Princeton, New Jersey

TO THE MEMORY OF
ROBERT J. MENNER

# preface

This edition of the Advent Lyrics of the Exeter Book attempts to study them, and to present their texts, as poems rather than as documents. They have been known, of course, for many years and have received a fair amount of attention from scholars in modern times. In their own time, however, a great deal of poetic skill and no small quantity of religious emotion went into their creation. A good ninety percent of the recent scholarly activity expended on them has been focused on their textual and linguistic problems, yet such activity, however interesting and important, should eventually become ancillary to an integrating literary interpretation.

During the last half of the nineteenth century, the lyrics were considered the first section (*Christ I*) of a tripartite poem by Cynewulf called the *Christ*. Some time ago the great majority of Old English scholars gave up this notion, which Dietrich in 1853 created almost out of whole cloth, and I shall not here enter into a controversy which men like Brandl, Trautmann, and Sisam have made a dead issue. As an independent poem, or group of poems, however, the Advent Lyrics have never been disengaged from Cynewulf, studied and edited alone and for themselves. The present edition proposes to do this.

The Exeter Book contains the most varied collection of Old English poems in existence, and it is so well known that I shall not give a description of the manuscript. It is imperfect at the beginning, and unfortunately the most illegible portions occur on the first pages of the poetry, precisely those containing the Advent Lyrics. At least one folio of the first gathering has been lost, because folio 14, the last folio of the gathering, has had its corresponding leaf (let us say x) cut off, although we can still see the stub of it. Thus the leaf originally preceding folio 8, on which the first poem now begins, undoubtedly contained the beginning of the first fragmentary lyric. There would have been room, perhaps, for another whole poem, beginning at the top recto of folio x, as well as the early part of the present Poem 1. This sort of speculation about the lost portion, however, is not likely to be fruitful, for it may perfectly well be that another whole gathering, now lost without trace, originally preceded this folio x.

There have not been frequent editions of the *Christ* as a whole; in fact, it was seldom edited except as part of a complete edition of the Exeter Book. The first edition was that of Benjamin Thorpe, whose *Codex Exoniensis* (1842), was a pioneer work in Old English editing. The entire MS was soon re-edited by C. W. Grein in his collection, *Bibliothek der angelsächsischen Poesie* (1857-1858). Forty years later Grein's *Bibliothek* was reworked completely by Richard Wülker, for whom Bruno Assmann edited the portion containing *Christ* (*Die Handschrift von Exeter*, 1898).

The first edition of *Christ* alone was published by Sir Israel Gollancz in 1892 (*Cynewulf's Christ*). Sir Israel was working at the time on a complete edition of the Exeter Book for the Early English Text Society, which, when it appeared, constituted a completely new editorial treatment of the poem. Of this complete edition, he lived to finish only the text and translation of the first part of the MS (*The Exeter Book*, EETS 104, 1895), and his projected introduction and notes to the poems never appeared.

The most important edition of these lyrics ever to appear was that of A. S. Cook (*The Christ of Cynewulf*, 1900). All later scholarship, and most especially the present effort, must acknowledge gratefully its debt to Cook's fine work. The places where it is out of date are far outnumbered by those where its contribution is permanent, and I have not hesitated to use his information where I could not improve on him. Often the problem is simply to shear away some of the overabundant material in Cook which is interesting but not immediately pertinent. Future students, however, will still be able to turn to his edition with considerable profit.

Only two editions of the poems have appeared since Cook's, and they both are of great textual importance: the Facsimile edition (*The Exeter Book of Old English Poetry*, 1933) and the third volume of the Krapp-Dobbie series, *The Anglo-Saxon Poetic Records* (*The Exeter Book*, 1936). Neither of these editions attempts a really critical treatment of the poems.

All the previous editions have contributed something, either to the text or to the interpretation of the poems, and I have consulted them all in preparing this edition. There have been several translations, also, which have been used. In addition, some four or five noteworthy studies of the poems have appeared during the last sixty years, as well as numerous smaller articles. Johannes Bourauel made a full-scale study of the sources of the series in the last years of the nineteenth century, and apparently he and Cook discovered independently the connection between the Advent O's and these poems ("Zur Quellen-und Verfasserfrage von Andreas Crist und Fata," *Bonner Beiblatt* 11, 1901, 65-132). He includes a great variety of material, but sometimes his "sources" are no more than works of slight similarity. Nevertheless his study does not deserve the complete neglect which later writers have accorded it.

Another valuable study, growing directly out of Cook's research, was that of Edward Burgert (*The Dependence of Part I of Cynewulf's Christ upon the Antiphonary*, 1921). In the 1930's, an Indian scholar, S. K. Das made an extensive study of the Cynewulfian poems, at the end of which he decided on metrical and stylistic grounds that the *Christ I* was not part of the genuine Cynewulf canon (*Cynewulf and the Cynewulf Canon*, 1942). More recently, Claes Schaar has written an excellent book on Cynewulf (*Critical Studies in the Cynewulf Group*, 1949), although unfortunately the Advent Lyrics are the poems he studies least profoundly. The most

*PREFACE*

sensitive critical treatment of these poems from a literary point of view is the brief discussion of C. W. Kennedy in his *The Earliest English Poetry* (New York, 1943).

In preparing this book, I have received help from many quarters, but most especially I want to express my gratitude to Professor Roland Smith of the University of Illinois, Professor D. W. Robertson of Princeton, Mr. Frank Francis of the British Museum, and Mrs. Audrey M. Erskine of the Chapter Library of Exeter Cathedral. I am also grateful to the superlative generosity of Princeton University for financial aid in various forms.

JACKSON J. CAMPBELL

*Princeton, N.J.*
*December 1958.*

## contents

| | |
|---|---|
| Preface | vii |
| Introduction | 1 |
|     The Advent Season | 3 |
|     Structure and Sources | 9 |
|     Date and Dialect | 36 |
| The Lyrics | 43 |
| Notes | 79 |
| Bibliography | 103 |
| Glossary and Word Index | 109 |

# the advent lyrics
# introduction

# the advent season

THERE can be no doubt that the Advent Lyrics are based very directly on a series of antiphons called the Advent O's. It can further be said with certainty that they owe a great deal in direct and indirect ways to the liturgical office for the Advent season in general. A brief explanation of that office is necessary, then, to an understanding not only of the doctrine but of the peculiar poetic quality of the poems.

The observance of Advent in the ninth and tenth centuries may not have been exactly the same as the modern practice in all respects, but it is unlikely that the spirit and tone of the season were greatly different.[1] The usage of the English church at this period was probably, though not certainly, the same as we find described in St. Gregory's *Liber Sacramentorum* and *Liber Responsalis*. Also the liturgical ideas and explanations of Amalarius of Trèves, as found in his *Liber de Ordine Antiphonarii*, were undoubtedly known throughout England after the early ninth century. Unfortunately, none of these early works is precise with regard to many details of procedure. The more distinctly English liturgy which we find well developed in the Sarum Missal and Breviary is far too late to be used for the period in question, since some of the textual readings as well as the practices described may have been adopted in the eleventh and early twelfth centuries.

Advent, as the season of preparation for the anniversary of Christ's birth, marks the opening of the Christian year. Depending on what day of the week Christmas falls, the exact date of the beginning of Advent varies from year to year, but as early as Gregory's *Liber Sacramentorum* we find that special Advent Masses, responds, and antiphons are provided for four Sundays before Christmas, as well as the week days

[1] Much of the discussion which follows is based on the great modern liturgical work of Dom Prosper Guéranger (*The Liturgical Year: Advent*, Dublin, 1867), simply because it is detailed and specific where none of the medieval sources are.

between.[2] In modern practice, the fourth of the special Sunday services is dropped if Christmas falls on Monday, and the service for the vigil of Christmas is substituted. Also, although Advent always has four Sundays, it is only when Christmas falls on Sunday that it contains four full weeks.

It is clear from Gregory's liturgical works that each Sunday and each week day during this season had its own particular service whose text differed slightly from the ordinary services of other times of the year. The antiphons, lessons, prefaces, and other variable parts of the service were all carefully chosen, not only to tell the story of Christ's birth but also to prepare the Christian spiritually for his participation in the full meaning of Christmas.

The over-all emotional tone of the Advent season is a curious mixture of joy and sadness. As in Lent, there is a consciousness of mankind's evil and the need of repentance for it, but at the same time there is rejoicing that Christ's incarnation provided the means of redemption. "The people are forcibly reminded of the sadness which fills the heart of the Church by the sombre colour of the Vestments. Excepting on the Feast of the Saints, purple is the only colour she uses; the Deacon does not wear the Dalmatic, nor the Subdeacon the Tunic. Formerly it was the custom, in some places, to wear Black Vestments. . . . In the Night Office, the Holy Church also suspends . . . the hymn of jubilation, *Te Deum Laudamus*. It is in deep humility that she awaits the supreme blessing which is to come to her; and in the interval she presumes only to ask, and entreat, and hope."[3] In the tenth century, Aelfric expressed an Old English approach to the season in

[2] According to Guéranger, p. 28, the oldest version of the *Liber Sacramentorum* provided for a five week Advent season, but by the ninth or tenth century it was reduced to four, and so appears in the great majority of MSS. Practices for the observance of Advent grew up slowly and varied greatly during the fifth, sixth, and seventh centuries, sometimes taking the form of a second Lent, with fasting and abstinence for as long as forty-three days. The growth of these practices is sketched by Cook, pp. xxvi-xxvii.

[5] Migne, *P.L.* 183, col. 45.

similar terms in one of his homilies, but at the same time he could also teach its more joyous side: "We sceolon eac Cristes acennednysse and his gebyrd-tide mid gastlicere blisse wurðian, and ūs sylfe mid gōdum weorcum geglengan, and us mid Godes lofsangum gebysgian, and ða ðing onscunian ðe Crist forbytt. . . ."[4]

As might be expected, the Middle Ages carefully classified and codified the multiple meanings of Advent, and the liturgy often forces the hearer to think of the event on several levels at once. The ambiguity thus produced does not introduce confusion, but rather allows a fuller and more profound experience. St. Bernard in the twelfth century expressed almost epigrammatically an ancient idea which is frequently visible in the Advent Lyrics: "Triplicem enim ejus adventum novimus: ad homines, in homines, contra homines."[5] This threefold coming means that the anniversary of Christ's actual, physical birth in Bethlehem was only the most elementary aspect of Christ's coming which the liturgy expressed. A second factor was the coming of Christ in a spiritual sense into the soul of each individual believer, and a third was an outgrowth of the second, the coming of Christ as judge.[6] The sober penitence of the season arose mainly from a recognition of this third meaning, with its overtones of the Second Coming and the Last Judgment; the joyful mood stemmed principally from the second.

The Gospel lesson for each of the four Sundays of Advent in the modern church stresses one aspect or another of the above ideas, and it is likely that the same was true at the time

---

[4] "Nativitas Domini," *The Homilies of the Anglo-Saxon Church*, II, ed. Benjamin Thorpe, p. 22.

[5] Migne, *P.L.* 183, col. 45.

[6] Dietrich recognized, but imperfectly understood, this sort of multiple meaning, and it led him to his theory that the first three poems in the Exeter Book were a single poem celebrating the "dreifache kommen Christi: die ankunft Cristi auf erden, seine himmelfahrt, seine wiederkunft zum gericht." See "Cynewulfs Crist," *Zeitschrift für deutsches Altertum* 9, p. 194.

*INTRODUCTION*

of these lyrics, but we are uncertain just what lessons were used in the ninth century. To illustrate the effect of the lessons, we can cite the modern practice of using Christ's prophesy of the Second Coming (Luke 21:25) for the Gospel on the first Sunday of Advent; this text forces a consciousness of Christ's coming to judge mankind at the same time one is thinking of the birth of Christ, and aids the believer's mind to encompass the whole of the meaning of Christ's mission to men. The *Praefatio* which introduces the *Sanctus* in the Mass was different each Sunday, too, and it led the participants into a perception of a variety of pertinent ideas as they prepared to communicate. Finally, special songs and antiphons were sung at appropriate times during both the Sunday services and the offices for the canonical hours, and they also brought out subtle and distinct aspects of Christ's coming to earth.

The *O*'s of Advent, so-called simply because they all begin with the exclamation *O*,[7] are one group of antiphons which the Church at least from the time of Gregory has given especial distinction. Although not in strictly poetic form, these short texts are distinctly poetic in conception, imagery, and tone. They are used at the hour of Vespers in connection with the canticle of Mary, the *Magnificat*, usually being sung once before and once after that text. Normally their use begins on December 17 and runs through December 23, on days called the Greater Ferias.[8] Exactly what the practice was in the ninth century we cannot be sure, but their connection with the Greater Ferias is made clear by Gregory in the *Liber Responsalis*, and we find in Amalarius confirmation for their use at the *Magnificat*. Their texts as given by Gregory are as follows:

> *O Sapientia! quae ex ore Altissimi prodüsti, attingens a fine usque ad finem fortiter, suaviter, disponensque omnia, veni ad docendum nos viam prudentiae.*

[7] By Amalarius called simply antiphons "*Quae in principio habent O*," *Studi e Testi*, Vatican City, 1950, p. 44.
[8] Guéranger, pp. 508ff. These dates are also those given by Amalarius, p. 155.

*O Adonai, dux domus Israel! qui Moysi in igne flammae rubi apparuisti, et ei in Sina legem dedisti, veni ad redimendum nos in brachio extento.*

*O radix Jesse! qui stas in signum populorum, super quem reges continebunt os suum quem gentes deprecabuntur, veni ad liberandum nos, jam noli tardare.*

*O clavis David, et sceptrum domus Israel! qui aperis et nemo claudit, claudis et nemo aperit, veni et educ vinctum de domo carceris, sedentem in tenebris, et umbra mortis.*

*O Oriens, splendor lucis aeternae et Sol justitiae! veni et illumina sedentem in tenebris et umbra mortis.*

*O Rex gentium et desideratus earum, lapisque angularis! qui facis utraque unum, veni, salva hominem quem de limo formasti.*

*O Emmanuel Rex et Legifer noster, exspectatio gentium et Salvator earum! veni ad salvandum nos, Dominus Deus noster.*

*O Virgo virginum! quomodo fiet istud, quia nec primam similem visa es, nec habere sequentem? Filiae Jerusalem, quid admiramini? Divinum est mysterium hoc quod cernitis.*[9]

*Orietur sicut sol Salvator mundi, et descendet in utero virginis sicut imber super gramen, alleluia.*[10]

Although in later times the first seven of these are sometimes referred to as the Seven Greater Antiphons, it is clear that Gregory did not limit the number to seven. As time went on, at least four other O antiphons became associated with the Greater Antiphons:

[9] This antiphon, addressed to the Virgin, is in modern practice sung on the Feast of the Expectation of the Virgin, which happens to fall on December 18, during the Greater Ferias. Burgert, p. 72, suggests that a different practice was followed in the Early Middle Ages, but he can only conjecture what that practice was. The Feast of St. Thomas, celebrated on December 21, also had its special antiphon *O Thoma Didyme*, but this does not enter into our discussion, since the Old English poet did not use it.

[10] Although not strictly speaking an *O*, this antiphon is included in Gregory's texts. Amalarius, p. 124, says it is sung at the *Benedictus* on the vigil of the Nativity.

*INTRODUCTION*

*O Gabriel, nuntius caelorum, qui januis clausis ad me intrasti, et verbum nuntiasti: Concipies et paries, Emmanuel vocabitur.*

*O Rex pacifice, tu ante saecula nate, per auream egredere portam, redemptos tuos visita, et eos illuc revoca unde ruerunt per culpam.*

*O mundi domina, regio ex semine orta, ex tuo jam Christus processit alvo, tamquam sponsus de thalamo; hic jacet in praesepio qui et sidera regit.*

*O Hierusalem, civitas Dei summi, leva in circuitu oculos tuos, et vide dominum tuum, quia jam veniet solvere te a vinculis.*

These additional O's first appear together with the Greater Antiphons in the Antiphonary of Hartker in the St. Gall MS 390, 391,[11] and are sometimes thought to be monastic additions to the group. When we compare the order and the composition of the lists of O antiphons in Gregory, Amalarius, and Hartker, we find that there must have been considerable variation in the use of these antiphons. At the time the Old English poems were written, it is likely that the number and order of the O antiphons were not rigidly fixed. The poet of the Advent Lyrics apparently used both the Greater O's and the Monastic O's indiscriminately, and, if the order which we find in the Exeter Book is his, he clearly followed his own fancy in arranging them.

[11] *Antiphonale du B. Hartker (Paléographie Musicale,* 2nd Series, 1), Solesmes, 1900. This MS has musical neums of an early type and is particularly valuable to the musicologist. It dates from about the year 1000, in no case later than 1017.

## structure and sources

In his useful study of the sources of the Advent Lyrics, Mr. Edward Burgert worked out a rather elaborate theory about the portion of this series which is lost at the beginning of the manuscript. He felt in the first place that the poet must have used all the *O* antiphons, and that since we do not seem to have lyrics based on the *O Sapientia, O Adonai,* and *O radix Jesse,* we must assume that poems based on those three antiphons were on the lost folios. Burgert sometimes seems to lose sight of the fact that his theory is conjectural, and I find it so doubtful as to be almost without value. When we consider the poet's methods as evidenced in the poems we do have, we get no clear indication that he ever planned to utilize all the antiphons in a systematic and comprehensive way. In the individual poems, the poet sometimes followed his sources closely, and at other times he wandered from them widely. He included at least four poems, vii, x, xi, xii, which are not based on either the Greater *O*'s or the Monastic *O*'s. With regard to the order of the poems he did base on antiphons, we find that the sequence in our series is like that of no other early medieval text of the *O* antiphons.[1] The Monastic antiphons are mixed with the Greater antiphons in such a way as to indicate that the poet made no real distinction between them, and cared little for the order he found in his antiphonary authorities,[2] if indeed he referred to any books at all.

The question next arises whether the poet, in rearranging

[1] Burgert, p. 65, compares the order of the poems with that of various antiphonaries. Whether or not the order of the poems as we have them is that of the poet or some later scribal editor is a matter on which we have no real evidence.

[2] We know very little about the uniformity expected in Church practice at this early period. It may indeed be that no rigid and fixed order was demanded, for Amalarius indicates that the practice in his church at Metz differed from that of Rome.

*INTRODUCTION*

the poems and using an order which he did not find in the antiphonary, was following some over-all plan of his own in order to give an organic unity to the series as a whole. In studying and comparing poem after poem, I have tried without success to find a rationale in the arrangement pattern of the twelve poems we have. One of the difficulties of earlier scholars who considered these lyrics as part of the larger *Christ* poem was that there is no narrative thread in these lyrics, as there is in *Christ II* and *Christ III*. As the poems are now viewed, of course, no narrative stream is required, but as we turn to other sorts of threads or connectives we are forced to the conclusion that there is no structural progression in idea or emotion from one poem to the next. There are, to be sure, certain recurring ideas which appear from time to time like *leit motifs*: the coexistence of the Father and the Son, the purity of Mary, the miracle of the virgin birth, Man's inability to understand God's mysteries, his misery and need for Grace, and the necessity for rendering abundant praise and glory to God. These themes appear irregularly, and weave themselves into no observable pattern of thematic structure, yet they do provide connecting links of a sort from poem to poem, and they, along with the obvious similarities of formal lyric structure, serve to unify the whole group. I conclude that the poet did not attempt any further architectonics in the construction of this collection of poems. Indeed there was no reason why he should. Like the series of antiphons which provided him with his basic idea, his poems can afford great aesthetic pleasure, can express devoted religious emotion, can serve as excellent indoctrination pieces, with no pretentions above those of a group of individual lyrics on the general subject of Christ's coming to earth. It may be coincidence that the poem which reaches the highest point of emotional intensity, number xi, occurs soon before the end of the collection, and thus invites our considering it as a climax to the series; it is most certainly not a coincidence that the last poem, number XII, was written with an air of finality which clearly indicates it was intended to terminate the series. Aside from these considerations, however, it is my opinion that the order of the poems is unimportant.

The structuring of the individual poem is a different matter, for the poet obviously intended to create small poetic unities. It is worthwhile, I think, to analyze the individual poems, partly for the purpose of critical explication and partly for investigating the methods of that *rara avis* in Old English literature, the lyric poet. In the fundamental outline of most of the poems, he follows the structure of the typical antiphon. The O antiphons are not all alike in structure, of course, but as Cook first remarked,[3] most of them contain an invocation or address at the beginning, a central section which refers, directly or obliquely, to some item of doctrine, and a petition requesting Christ's visit to earth. The Old English poet assimilated this skeleton structure so thoroughly that he carried it over even into poems based on antiphons which differ in structure; in *Eala þu mæra*, for instance, he adds a petition section, although the antiphon *O mundi domina* does not have one. This basic structure is perhaps the most important thing the antiphons contributed to the Old English poems, for the poet, as will be seen in the individual analyses, more often than not elaborated, compressed, supplemented, or otherwise modified the material he found in the Latin text. So often did he make free with the antiphons, in fact, that there are very few cases where we can say with justice that the poem paraphrases the antiphon.

POEM I. The decapitation of the first poem does not obscure the fact that the poet was working with an extended metaphor concerned with architecture, building, and creation. Kennedy[4] alone among the critics of the poem seems to have noticed

[3] Cook, pp. xli-xlii.
[4] C. W. Kennedy, *The Earliest English Poetry*, New York, 1943, p. 238.

it, although the image is pervasively present and probably was introduced even earlier in the portion which is lost. Its origins, of course, are Biblical, for *weallstān* quite evidently comes from the antiphonal phrase *lapis angularis*, which in turn comes from Ephesians II, where Paul in turn was drawing on the Psalms, Isaiah, and other Old Testament passages in which the allegorical significance of the cornerstone image is well developed. The Old English poet gathers both the Old and New Testament suggestions together and orders them in such a way as to make the building metaphor the structuring principle of his poem.

Christ is the *weallstān* which the workers of old discarded from the building, but immediately we must pause, for each of these terms admits of several interpretations. A building (*healle mǣre*) was a frequent metaphor for Christ's Church, either temporal or eternal. The workers could be the Jews who crucified Christ or those who built their religion without Christ's spirit.[5] Possibly they are churchmen who make the Church a thing devoid of that spirit, or perhaps even the individual sinner who shapes his own life and personality after rejecting Christ. However one interprets these lines, of course, the action of the *wyrhtan* is egregiously ironic, for Christ, rejected or not, *is* the head, the keystone of creation and all created things. He it is who holds the walls together into one building, who makes a firmly joined unity out of multiplicity. The syntax of lines 5 and 6 brings out this idea rather cleverly: *gesomnige* has two direct objects, *weallas*, plural, and *flint*, not only unbroken but grammatically singular.

The metaphor is picked up and carried a step further as the petition begins in line 9. The poet requests that Christ reveal his work, make clear his unifying presence in all things, thus leaving wall against wall, or wall connected to wall, in such a way that they are no longer disparate and alien, but

---

[5] This common interpretation appears in Old English literature in a homily of Aelfric (Thorpe's *Catholic Homilies* II, 580-582).

held together as part of a single structure. *Wið* in Old English can carry the sense of opposition or the meaning of accompaniment, and in this passage it seems that either or both meanings add significance.

The word *weorc* appears three times in these seventeen lines. Its meaning seems at first rather generalized, something like "created object" or perhaps "process and operation of creation." This vagueness leaves us free to interpret the metaphor of which it is a part in a broad way; the lines certainly achieve very distinct effects if you think of the *weorc* as some aspect of the external world or as man's internal world. I remark this vagueness without inferring criticism on the poet; actually, he has taken even more general and abstract words (*facis utraque unum*) and given them at least some specific visual imagery. At line 14, he becomes slightly more definite: the *weorc* is the *hrā*, the body of man whose limbs God made of clay. The *wergan hēap* of the next line widens the concept to mean collective mankind. As we pin the meaning down to "man," we notice that the ending of the poem reflects back on the sections whose meaning was vague. Man, it appears, is the *hūs* which is decaying, the hall whose walls have a tendency to fall apart. A certain amount of paradox is therefore present in the entire poem, for on the one hand the *weorc* at line 9 is admirable and glorious, but at line 13 the house is greatly in need of betterment. Naturally, the poet is only expressing in a new way the ancient Christian paradox of the coexistence of both God's image and original sin in man.

*POEM II.* This poem is far from being a paraphrase of *O clavis David*, for only lines 2-3 and 8-9 bear any close resemblance to the antiphon. Some of the finest things in the Latin text, such as the neat rhetorical repetition and reversal in the doctrine section, apparently did not interest the poet at all. The metaphor of the key—the first point which he drew

## INTRODUCTION

from the antiphon—he makes somewhat more explicit; it is *līf*, in its full spiritual meaning, which is opened, and the beautiful paths of heaven which are closed to those whose works are faulty. The two concepts are virtually synonymous.

At line 9, the poet begins to expand the antiphon rather freely. The words *in tenebris et umbra mortis* he turns inside out in order to create a vivid passage concerned with light. The line *hwonne ūs Līffrēa/ lēoht ontȳne* looks like a conscious development and amplification of *līf ontȳneð* in line 2. The concepts of life and Lord and light are subtly intertwined in this line by the alliterative pattern, and their association is firmly emphasized before the poet takes up other matters. Instead of following the antiphon in putting stress on the dark imprisonment of our present state, the poet next shifts his focus to the bright future (*sunnan wēnað*). His forward-looking fervor takes the form of optative verbs, *weorðe* and *bewinde*, and reaches an emotional climax in the words *tīre* and *wuldre*, words which not only suggest visual light in an intense degree, but also much of the magnificence and mystic emotion of the term "glory" in its full religious force.

The imperfect text of lines 6 and 7 makes dogmatic assertion unwise, but it certainly appears that the poet recast the entire petition section of the antiphon, substituting a series of optative verbs for the imperative *veni et educ*. The tone which is established by these verbs in lines 8-13 is one of hope and expectation, searching and yearning, but as the section ends (lines 14-15) the tone subsides to a rueful matter-of-factness.

The poet's freedom with the antiphons is nowhere more obvious than in the second half of this poem. Here he adds a doctrine section after the petition, and it begins at line 16 in an especially low key:

> Forþon secgan mæg       sē ðe sōð spriceð
> þæt hē āhrēdde,         þā forhwyrfed wæs,
> frumcyn fīra.

## STRUCTURE AND SOURCES

This rather flat, narrative mode seems almost like the summation after a passage of argument. The lines which follow are also declarative, stating several facts in a more or less straightforward way. The virgin Christ chose to be his mother was young; she conceived without sexual intercourse with a man. As the poet dwells on the concept of the virgin birth, however, his imagination is gradually quickened, and at about line 20 or 21 a heightened emotion is injected into the poetry. There is an awe and a marveling at the secret and mysterious nature of the miracle.

This heightened poetry is maintained to the end of the poem, as the poet mentions the spiritual gifts made possible by this birth, and the way in which this mystery explains other mysteries. The dark and difficult sayings of so many old prophets are now made clear; they come to life like seeds that have been waiting under the soil until a spirit of life is breathed into them. The extended and well-developed metaphor in this passage has not been noted by previous editors, for *wīsna* was taken as the adjective *wīs*, wise. Read as the noun *wīse*, sprout, seedling, it fits nicely, along with the words *geondsprēot*, *hoðman* and *biholen* into the metaphor of the life-giving words of the prophets.

At first glance, the break at line 16 seems to split the poem into two unrelated sections. The ideas and themes treated by the poet in the latter half have very little to do with the *O clavis David*, to be sure, but the poet was still working his own poem toward a unity. We can see that he has seized upon one suggestion from the antiphon, condensed the rest, and, following only roughly the general idea of the Latin, finally set off on his own to expand by means of his own metaphor a notion which caught his fancy. The process must not have been a haphazard one where one thought led loosely to another, for the whole poem makes good use of all its parts. In the integral poem, he is interested in developing an idea connected, through the light imagery, with man's understanding. The

*INTRODUCTION*

request in the petition is that God should reveal to us His light, become a patron to our minds (*mōde*). In the second half, the poet explores the historical event which represents that light. The birth of Christ had a special meaning for the later readers of the Hebrew prophets, those *wita* whose old lore was obscure and dark to men's minds until the coming of Christ. By Him their words were illumined (*inlihted*), or rather our understanding of them was illumined. This was accomplished, the poet insists, by the originator of life and light (*Līffrea, līfes Fruman*), whose action not only brought life to the *wōðsong* of the prophets, but also enlightens and enlivens us and our *tydre gewitt*. What the poet has done, then, is not to paraphrase badly an antiphon but to create an original and unified poem of his own, starting from a bare suggestion in the antiphon.

*POEM III.* The poem *Eala sibbe gesihð* stays as close to the antiphon on which it is based as any poem in the series, but even here the poet contributes enough of his own personality to keep it from being a pedestrian paraphrase. The poem opens with a thoroughly medieval touch in that the name Jerusalem is first explained according to the meaning of its component elements. The poem then proceeds in a thoroughly Old English fashion as the poet expands *civitas dei* into a series of parallel phrases, some of which might be considered kennings. The term *burglond* must be classed as one of the happier transferences of native English terms and concepts to Christian contexts.

Perhaps the most important single thing the poet has done is, as Cook first noted, to explore three, or perhaps four, of the allegorical interpretations of Jerusalem. Besides the heavenly Jerusalem, which is apparently the subject of the opening address, and the earthly Jerusalem of the Church and the body of human believers which is manifestly referred to in the closing lines, the central portion of the poem seems

{ 16 }

## STRUCTURE AND SOURCES

also to use the Virgin Mary as one of the significations of the term. This bit of allegory goes back at least as far as the commentaries of Athanasius, and is ultimately based on such Biblical passages as Psalms 131:13 and Canticle of Canticles 6:3. The lines

>     Næfre wommes tācn
> in þam eardgearde    ēawed weorþeð,
> ac þē firena gehwylc    feor ābūgeð

are clearly the poet's own addition to the *O Hierusalem* antiphon, and they were probably added to strengthen the connection with the spotless purity of the Blessed Virgin and to broaden the significance of the central symbol. A little later, the words *ond sylf cymeð/ nimeð eard in þē* have a clear meaning if we take the *þē* to refer to the Virgin Mary, in whose womb He began His earthly existence, as well as to the city of the Jews, or to the Church in which Christ always lives, or to the soul of the devout man.[6]

There can be no doubt that the poet has enriched the material found in the antiphon by forcing our overt awareness of multiple significances existing simultaneously in the words of the liturgical text.

At the close of the poem, we have a fine statement of one of the most persistent of the recurrent themes in the series, namely the miserable state of *ūs*, the sinners awaiting and wanting Christ's advent. Throughout these poems we have reflections of the dual time consciousness of the Christian worshipper. Although he knows that the advent of Christ occurred in the past and that man already has been saved by Christ's sacrifice, yet for the individual man salvation and Christ's advent into his soul is always a fervently wished-for future event. The poet speaks in the term *wē* for himself, his audience, and all waiting Christians. Variations on this theme appear and reappear in many of these poems, and provide

---

[6] See the quotation from Rhabanus Maurus, p. 85.

*INTRODUCTION*

one of the threads of unifying idea and tone for the whole series. In terms of emotional effect in the poems, this technique is especially important. Since these lyrics are essentially didactic, the character of the *persona* of the poet as a vulnerable and imperfect sinner not only allows the poems to escape a sanctimonious and magisterial tone, but also adds the positive factor of personal emotion which promotes the audience's participation in them.

*POEM IV.* The antiphon O *virgo virginum* differs from most of the other antiphons in being written in a simple dialogue form. The pattern of address, doctrine, and petition is therefore absent, but we can see that the Old English poet, in typical fashion, has added a certain amount of doctrine and conventional teaching as he expanded the rather bare question and answer of the antiphon. In general, he has followed his original with some degree of fidelity, but as always he betrays his peculiar enthusiasms. Here, as in several other spots in these lyrics, he displays a lively fascination with the idea of the eternal virginity. The Latin text lets the idea be implicit in the pronoun *istud*, but the Old English poet spends ten lines (5 to 15a) making it clearer and clothing it in a tone of wonder. At the close of the first speech, he goes on to adapt a folk phrase (*sorgum sāwað,/ swā eft rīpað*), drawn ultimately from the Epistle to the Galatians, and applies it in a novel context, contrasting the glory of this particular birth with ordinary conception and birth, thus emphasizing Mary's superiority to ordinary mankind.

Mary's answer to the sons and daughters of Salem seems at first to have a slightly reproving tone, perhaps even sharper than that indicated in the Latin text. As she continues, her tone becomes patient and explanatory as she expounds the ancient doctrine of Mary's love compensating for Eve's guilt. This idea introduces a feeling of exultation and fervor, almost as if her own imagination were caught up by the blessing and glory which she is making possible to women as well as men. The poet works this tone smoothly into the conventional close, with its formulaic air of termination.

*POEM V.* This poem demonstrates some of the most typical techniques of the Old English poet, and also betrays some of his most salient weaknesses. By comparing his poem with the Latin source, we see that he has killed most of the poetry of the antiphon. The first half of the antiphon, with its vocative nouns, produces an effect of fervency and adoration. The second half, with its imperative *veni* and *ilumina*, creates a tone of urgent pleading and supplication. The Old English poem turns these rather powerful emotional effects into poetry of statement. Even the opening *Ēalā* sentence is eventually resolved at line 5 by a declaratory present indicative verb.

The antiphon and the first half of the poem where the poet follows the antiphon elaborate the common metaphor, God is light. There is contrasting darkness imagery in the petition section, and this imagery the poet makes explicit as the spiritual darkness of sin. Throughout this poem, and indeed in many poems through the series, we see the poet filling out suggestive symbols and images with phrases containing standard theological ideas. Sources for these ideas are usually not to be sought, for they are in most cases religious commonplaces. From the hint in the word *aeternae* issues the doctrine of Christ's coexistence with the Father (*gēaro ācenned*).

After the poet completes his paraphrase of the antiphon at line 15, he adds an original section, amounting to almost half of the total poem, in which he repeats the ideas of the first half by applying them more specifically to men on earth. He transforms *splendor* from the *engla beorhtast* into *flǣsc*. Christ is at once the Word which has always existed and also the human being born of Mary at a specific time in history. The poet's love for stressing the Christian paradoxes is revealed

*INTRODUCTION*

in his statement that Christ's divine nature and his human nature dwelt together in harmony here on earth. Christ's advent as comforter to an imprisoned mankind (*gēomrum tō gēoce*) not only brings hope but it also obligates man, as the poet soberly concludes, to a life of thanksgiving as shown in his works. Although the technique of supplementing and amplifying source material from conventional and standard doctrine can at times be handled very felicitously by our poet, it seems that in *Ēalā Ēarendel* the ardor of his imagination was not called into sufficient play.

*POEM VI.* This poem begins a little breathlessly as the poet dwells on the meaning of the word Emmanuel. Etymological explanation of Hebrew words was a frequent practice among the writers of the books of the Greek New Testament, and it was taken up enthusiastically by most of the learned men of the Middle Ages. It is understandable enough that the poet's attention should shift in line 6 to the prophets who foretold Christ's coming, for the name Emmanuel is explained and elaborated in the Book of Isaiah, one of the greatest of the prophets of Christ's coming. The *gomel* he treats at length, however, is Melchisedech rather than Isaiah. Melchisedech throughout the Middle Ages was taken as a prototype of Christ, and in that he was an earlier manifestation of Christ's very spirit, he revealed God's glory in a very special way. Historically, he was a contemporary of Abraham, and the idea of the *legifer* or *ǣ bringend* carries at least slight overtones of God's agent Moses and his early revelation of the law; perhaps it is the thought of these venerable patriarchs who lived before the incarnation that accounts for the curiously effective thing the poet does next.

The petition of the antiphon is similar to that of several others in the group, *veni ad salvandum nos*. This request is usually conceived as coming from the mouths of a group of living human beings, the miserable *wē*, which group includes the poet and his audience. The poet has introduced a motif from the story of the Harrowing of Hell, however, and puts the petition into the mouths of the righteous dead in limbo awaiting the liberation of Christ's visit to hell. This shift is clear from the word *grundas* in line 16, and the third person *hīe* in line 17. For centuries one of the most common metaphors applied to humanity in its fallen state had been that of bondage; it occurs frequently in both the Old and New Testaments, and in the O antiphons it looms large in *O clavis David* and *O Hierusalem*. The sadness, the torments, the fetters, and all the other images and emotions connected with this metaphor can easily be applied to the souls in hell with greatly increased effect. The terms *hæftas*, *wītepēow*, and *brynetēar*, as well as the concepts of chains, tortures, and weariness, all of which had long since assumed a very conventional air, achieved a new force and a more convincing meaning when applied to the souls of the patriarchs awaiting Christ. Perhaps it is because the other poems reflect on this one, and this petition sounds like many of the others, but we are conscious throughout this portion of the poem that the *wē* theme is being expanded. The souls in hell and the suffering community of living sinners become one, and there is a great intensification of the meaning and the emotion of the poem.

As the Old English poet prays for Christ's mercy, he does something which is altogether characteristic of him. Praise for God and reveling in His glory are never far from his lips, and from line 30 to the end, as his focus shifts from the petitioners to the glory of God, the tone changes from gloom to exultation. These lines leave the impression that stopping the pain of humanity is not the reason adduced for mercy and salvation so much as allowing humanity to praise and glorify God properly. The poem ends with a short sentence, close in feeling to the *Gloria in Excelsis Deo*, of simple faith and praise.

*INTRODUCTION*

Although constructed out of the most diverse elements, this poem becomes one of the most successful of the entire series. Even to modern ears, it does not fly apart into incoherent and incompatible parts; there are connections between each section and the next, tenuous perhaps, but not unintelligible. What holds the whole together and leaves the reader with the feeling that there is real unity in this rather rambling structure is the attitude of the poet toward God, an attitude of fresh, optimistic, enthusiastic praise from beginning to end.

*POEM VII*. The strong dramatic element in this poem has led several critics to make rather extravagant claims for a form of vernacular drama in England as early as the ninth century. This notion has gained no widespread acceptance, but many readers tend to overestimate the dramatic element and miss the true quality and extent of the originality of the poem. The dialogue form makes it unusual in this series, although *Ēalā wīfa wyn* could perhaps be considered as a rudimentary example of the same genre, yet it is not sufficiently different from the other poems to make us suspect an interpolation from the mind of a different poet. Even were it not for certain correspondences of style and several appearances of our poet's favorite themes, the fundamental purpose and direction of the poem reveal it as one of the didactic lyrics of this particular poet.

The entire piece consists of only five brief speeches, but the poet achieves his effects quickly and economically. Mary's first speech establishes the situation, making clear that we are picking up the story at the time when Joseph has confronted her with his resolve to "put her away privily," but has not yet explained why. In these three and a half lines the poet not only accomplishes his exposition but reveals something of Mary's character, her love for Joseph, and her questioning, bewildered feeling at this moment in the face of his announcement.

When we consider the structural plan the author had in mind for this little dialogue, Joseph's answer to Mary seems extremely skillfully written. He reveals his deep sorrow and his troubled state of mind, but he is not entirely explicit about its cause, and some suspense is created as we wait for Mary's comprehension. He does state that he has suffered *tornworda fela* for her, so we assume that some sort of gossip or talk of other men is responsible for his distress. In the midst of his sorrow, however, we see his complete faith in God and in His healing power. He also has a good deal of residual faith in Mary, and his closing cry (lines 12b-13a) expresses his tortured reluctance to believe what his reason tells him must be his beloved's dishonor. This final cry also confirms the effect of grieving confusion and partial incoherence which exists throughout his speech.

In Mary's rejoinder, we see that she has missed the words *for þē* of line 6, and indeed has missed the point of his entire speech. She thinks he is bemoaning some sin of his own, yet she declares he has always been admirable and upright; she simply does not understand. This misunderstanding not only allows the poet to bring in outside testimony of Joseph's good character, but it reinforces our conviction of Mary's innocence and simplicity. The possibility of the sort of infidelity which Joseph has in mind has never entered her thoughts, so that even when given such a strong hint, she does not comprehend it.

Joseph's distress is explained much more clearly in his next speech, and everywhere it is evident that his deep love for Mary is the thing that makes his a true dilemma. Part of his trouble is the simple matter of the injured pride of a man enduring the jibes of other men about the chastity of his wife. He has a masculine need to strike back, to fire back some sort of answer, but he cannot honestly find any ammunition to

## INTRODUCTION

use. This touch of insight into Joseph's psychology is down-to-earth and human, to be sure, but it is by no means introduced for its own sake. Any naturalism in the poem is subordinated to its doctrinal purposes. Joseph's real problem is a moral one. He must choose between delivering up the woman he loves to justice and death, and concealing a crime, thereby both committing a kind of personal dishonesty and allowing the criminal to live happily unpunished among human kind. His struggle is between his deepest personal desires and his strongest convictions of a moral nature.

This second speech of Joseph's, although not completely explicit, at least makes clear to Mary just what it is that he suspects. She is not shocked or hurt, but rather she seems figuratively to step forward in a ceremonious and impressive way to clear up Joseph's doubts, to clarify an item of doctrine, and to end the whole poem on a note of glorifying God. The poet, in order to make Mary's climactic speech more emphatic, puts in a line and a half of introduction to her speech, written in the narrative mode.[7] Her speech certainly removes all doubts about the structure, focus, and purpose of the entire poem. From the beginning it has been built up gradually to this climax—from Mary's initial wonder, through the two stages of Joseph's gradual revelation of his doubts, to Mary's realization and explanation of the mystery of the virgin birth and her eternal virginity. The factors which tend to interest the twentieth-century sensibility most, namely the characterization of the two speakers and Joseph's emotional struggle, were unquestionably subordinate elements in the mind of the Old English poet. Further, it is best not to apply dramatic criteria of judgment to Mary's last speech, lest she appear

[7] It is merely the absence of these speech introductions that has lead people to entangle themselves in dramatic theories about the poem. If the other speeches were thus introduced, this would be a fragment of conversation not greatly different from many we have in the Old English narrative poems. The neat organization of the five speeches into a small unity, however, is neither a narrative nor a dramatic technique, but a lyric one.

prudish and pretentious as a woman. As a spokesman for religious instruction, she fulfills her function in the poem admirably, for the dignity of the teacher is more to the purpose than the appealing ingenuousness of the young girl. A poet trying to convey the truth of an idea would consider complete consistency of characterization in a case like this a matter of letting the tail wag the dog. Although this poem is cast in a mold very different from that of the surrounding lyrics, it achieves a remarkable success in its novel form. The poet has very skillfully used elements of character, suspense, and rising action, but has kept them all in proper proportion to contribute to his essentially didactic end.

*POEM VIII.* One of the most interesting aspects of this lyric is the sort of elaboration the poet gives to the phrase *tu ante saecula nate*. The idea of Christ's coexistence with the Father, or as it is sometimes called, the eternal generation of the Son, is an important one, of course, to hold in mind simultaneously with the vision of the nativity at Bethlehem, in order to prevent an erroneous and sentimental conception of the birth of Christ. For this particular poet, however, it appears that this idea provided an especially potent stimulus to the imagination, as potent as that provided by the notion of Mary's eternal virginity in other poems. It recurs several times in the series, though never as emphatically and excitedly as it stands in this lyric. In order to vivify the concept of Christ's existence before all created things, the poet paraphrases a few verses from the first chapter of Genesis. He and his audience, if they sent their imaginations back through time, came inevitably to the creation story in Genesis as the earliest of all events, and the first act of God was of course the creation of light. It is highly dramatic, then, to say that even before this act, Christ was. As the poet continues, he carries the dramatic element a stage further by adding another bit of

## INTRODUCTION

doctrine: Christ not only existed before the creation, but he is the *Sapientia* which effected the work of creation.

In this section, as the poet dwells on what for him was a stimulating idea, he uses another very effective technique for emphasis. In lines 6 and following he stresses the mystery and the marvel of the eternal generation, the fact that men, even the most intelligent, cannot understand this phenomenon. The wording here is similar to that in other poems where he underlines man's inability to comprehend the mystery of the virgin birth. Lines 6 to 10 not only exhibit a rhetorical pattern which virtually amounts to one of the formulae of Old English poetry, but also reveal a favorite and typical manner of thought with this particular poet; similar passages occur in II 22-23, IV 24-25, and XII 6-7. He used the same thought, and the same formula, again only a few lines farther along (lines 28ff.). It may perhaps be felt that the poet weakens his point by using this element, so slightly disguised, twice in the same poem; perhaps his religious enthusiasm has led him into literary crudity. This modern attitude, I am sure, would not appear in the poet's time, and the poetic effect was probably felt to be one of incremental emphasis.

The petition section of the poem presumably starts with the *Cum nū* at line 30b, but the poet is not quite ready to drop the idea which occupied him in the doctrine section. He lingers until line 35 on our inability to understand Christ's paternity. The bulk of the petition is concerned with our fall from Grace and our need for help. As in the antiphon, there is little connection, either in imagery or idea, between the doctrine and the petition. The phrase *per auream portam* receives some expansion, part of which is possibly drawn from another antiphon, *O clavis David*. Here, however, he connects the closing of the gates with the expulsion from paradise. Perhaps this story introduced to the poet's mind the idea of mankind's enemy. As he proceeds to depict the devil as an active force, the blame for mankind, implicit in *per culpam*, is dissipated.

Part of this effect is doubtless caused by the conventional imagery the poet accepts from the Bible. The wolf and flock analogy makes the individual sheep seem as blameless as he is helpless. There is little indication of a personal acceptance of guilt here such as we see in the poem *Ēalā þū hālga* (x 15).

After the suggestion of the expulsion from paradise, there is some indication that the scene shifts to hell until the end of the poem. The petition of this poem, like that of *Ēalā gǣsta god*, seems to be spoken by people who are at the same time living human beings and inhabitants of hell. These *hellbūend*, however, are far from despairing. Laced through their complaints about the devil are references to Christ's saving action and to our dependence upon His Grace. The audience never loses sight of the poet's confidence that Christ will forestall our eternal damnation.

*POEM IX.* If it were not for the phrase *cwēn ofer eorðan*, it might be disputed that *O mundi domina* is the source of this poem at all. So different is it in structure and idea, we can only believe that the poet used the antiphon for little more than an opportunity to write another poem on the Virgin. It is curious that much of the most effective and poetic material in the Latin was not touched by the poet, yet from some few hints of idea (like the phrase *tuo alvo*), he constructs elaborate and lengthy perorations.

The first section of the poem, lines 1 to 26, is filled with excited, almost ecstatic praise of the Virgin and her purity. The poet presents the situation as if a fair exchange were accomplished in choosing Mary as the mother of Christ; she had tendered her chastity and maidenhood to God, and in consequence he took her for his bride and sent Gabriel to perform the annunciation. At the end of this section, the poet mentions the fact that Mary should always thenceforth be virginally *unwemme*. This mystery never failed to fire the

## INTRODUCTION

imagination of our poet, and here it sends him off on the long central section, built around the metaphor of the locked gate. In terms of imagery, the simile of the *sponsus ex thalamo* is dropped, although the idea remains in the metaphor of the *auream portam*. This latter image, for the third time in the series, is dwelt on at length. Since the vision of Ezekiel concerning the splendors of the temple had in early Old Testament commentary been interpreted as a prophecy referring to Mary and the virgin birth, the poet's train of thought is not surprising. Of the great wealth of material in the four chapters of Ezekiel dealing with the temple, the poet chose only that which concerned his locked-gate metaphor, and thus in the midst of a rich profuseness of description, he keeps the emphasis on the miraculous birth and the eternal virginity. The beauty of the gate is clearly visualized as the poet adapts phrase after phrase from the standard Old English poetic vocabulary (e.g. lines 34-36), but attention is never allowed to stray to the other details, many of them fascinating, which Ezekiel saw in the temple. Throughout this central portion of the poem, the poet maintains the tone of wonder and mystery at the marvelous vision. The strangeness of seeing (*scēawode, wlāt, gestarode*) great spaces and great beauty prepares for the awe of hearing words of revelation from one of God's angels. At line 54 the poet returns to the intimate, respectful, and adoring tone of the first section, as he shifts back to Mary and explains the symbolism of the vision. As he does so, some of the splendor of the golden-gate imagery and the strength and finality of the lock imagery transfer themselves to our attitude toward the Virgin.

The invention of a petition section for a poem containing this particular material required some ingenuity on the part of the poet. He adapted the pattern of the other antiphons with skill, however, and put the matter on a basis of Mary's intercession with her Son for our salvation. In line 67, *nū wē on þæt bearn foran brēostum stariað*,[8] we find the only spot in these twelve Christmas poems where the intimate and slightly sentimental image of the mother and child is insisted upon. The poet's interest is most often on the glorious, the awe-inspiring, and the transcendent rather than the sentimental. The advent of Christ on earth, as reflected in these lyrics, is always an earnest, adult matter which affects in a serious manner the nature and direction of the intellectual and spiritual, as well as the emotional, lives of men on earth.

*POEM X.* The two parts of this poem are quite well worked up, but there is very little cohesive force between them aside from the fact that they are both about Christ. Burgert suggested that this poem is the poet's "own *O*," or an original poem written in the pattern of the other *Ēalā* poems. He further showed that the poet drew the core of the first section of the poem from the preface to the Midnight Mass on Christmas.[9] These proposals seem entirely cogent and acceptable to me, and they partially explain the rather loose structure of the poem. The poet here, setting out to write a poem on his own, had the opportunity to bring in at will several of his favorite ideas. He echoes in the central section a passage of the Christmas Mass which had particularly appealed to him, but since he also has to have a petition section, he again brings in ideas and images from the many *O*'s which he had been using as source material in earlier poems.

Cook uses the term "contamination" when the poet, presumably paraphrasing one antiphon, draws in material from another. In so far as this word has pejorative connotations, it is probably inappropriate, for this process is actually one of the virtues of the poet. His mind was filled with phrases and attitudes not only from all eleven antiphons but also from

---

[8] I cannot understand why Burgert found this line "in agreement with" *hic jacet in praesepio* (p. 32), nor why *in Fæder rīce* "points to" *qui et sidera regit*.

[9] Burgert, p. 41.

the daily and Sunday office as well. He made no great effort to separate them and keep them in their proper compartments. They appear in the poems as his processes of association call them up, and we should not be surprised to find, for example, images or ideas from one antiphon in the poem based on another, for he had so thoroughly assimilated the antiphons that they would issue from his mind into his poems in an ordering which was his. The idea of the eternal generation of the Son could have come, as Burgert suggests, from the Preface to the Mass, or it could have come from the *O Sapientia* or from *O Rex pacifice*; in all probability the poet could not have distinguished which.

Throughout the second half of the poem, the imagery of misery and bondage, drawn from any one of four antiphons, is used again and again. It is surprising that this plethora of words connoting pain, poverty, misery, and humiliation, all applied to the *wē* group for whom the poet is speaking, does not produce a tone of special pleading and self-pity. The edge, I think, of a "poor us" feeling is taken off by the simultaneous presentation of the idea that "it is our own fault." Here the poet was perhaps reaching into the general confession for the *mea culpa* theme. We are afflicted and unhappy *þurh ūre sylfra gewill*. The fiend has bound us and made us slaves, not so much through his action as through our own: *wē fǣhþo wið þē/ þurh firena lust gefremmed hæbben*. Implied here is a sophisticated concept of the nature of evil which is neither weak nor superstitious.

Another factor which influences the emotional content of the lines away from the impression of maudlin self-pity is the earnest tone of sincere supplication running through the petition. At the beginning we have the simple and straightforward *Wē þē . . . biddað*; shortly thereafter the complete dependence of suffering mortals on the gift of Grace is acknowledged (*Is sēo bōt gelong/ eall æt þē ānum; ūs hǣlogiefe/ sōðfæst sylle*). Since there is throughout an under-

## STRUCTURE AND SOURCES

current of firm faith and assurance that His Grace will be forthcoming, no feeling of groveling is produced. In fact, a certain dignity and strength is conferred on the speaker even while he is confessing to weakness and humiliation. The directness and urgency of the plea *Cym nū, hǣleþa Cyning/ ne lata tō lange*, with all its vulnerability and faith, destroy any tendency to a maudlin tone. The closing lines quietly and earnestly tie up the two elements of the petition, the misery and the remedy, by a nice repetition and balance: the *hǣlogiefe* of Christ's advent will permit us to do *þīnne willan*, which leads to *sellan þing* than the results of doing *ūre sylfra gewill*.

POEM XI. My objection to Cook's two Trinity antiphons as the source for this poem lies principally in my belief that this is not basically a poem about the Trinity. To be sure, the *þrȳness* at line 2 is the subject of the opening address, but at no other point in the poem is the three-in-one nature of the Deity mentioned or developed. Certainly no reference to the distinct persons in the Godhead is made so specific as it is in the preceding poem (x 10-11). At line 6, Christ is said to have revealed the nature of God (the Father?), but the poet insists on no trinitarian application of his terms. At line 14 *Cyninge* apparently refers to the Father, and *Crist* certainly to the Son, but nowhere is the Holy Spirit mentioned. Later in the poem various names are used for God, some of which traditionally apply to the Father, some to the Son (*Waldend, Frēa, Dryhten, Nergend*), but the poet does not make a point that these separate entities are the same entity. The poet's terminology for the Godhead is loose and varied, as was that of most Old English poets, and it is far too imprecise for anything as technical as the paradoxical mystery of the Trinity. In this poem, as everywhere else in this series of lyrics, trinitarian doctrine is pervasively present in the sense that the poet undoubtedly believed it, and habitually thought

*INTRODUCTION*

of the *Nergend* and the *Waldend* as the same essence, but he did not make that doctrine the theme of this poem.

The ideas and the feelings which the poet drew from the Preface as he heard, or perhaps said, the Mass, he transformed into a poem on the general subject of praise—praise for the Godhead in general, without reference to the distinct persons comprised in it. The verbs *hergan, brēman, weorðian,* and *lofian* occur throughout the poem; the noun *weorðmynd* occurs in the first line and *herenis* in the last. In its structure, a contrast is definitely made between men and angels with regard to the matter of their praise of God. At the beginning the *eorðware* are praising God on the *brytenwongas* of this earth, but the poet speaks of these mortal *reordberend* as *earme*. There is further a suggestion in the phrase *ealle mægene* that they have some difficulty in praising God properly. The *Hælend* revealed God to us in order that we can in a sense know him, but that knowledge seems only dark and imperfect when compared with the knowledge of the angels, who enjoy God's presence face to face.

The middle section of the poem (lines 8-25) makes use of idealized and imaginative imagery of the flight and caroling of the *seraphinnes cynn*, drawn from various passages from the Bible and Biblical commentary. The general picture of the angels here is highly conventional, but the use made of it is perfectly adapted to the poet's unique ends, and thus becomes original. Points of similarity and contrast between the angels and men are subtly established. Angels also are *reordberend* and they sing praises with loud, sweet voices. Their praise is joyous, unwearied, and accompanied with a certain gaiety. As they flutter and throng about God, protecting his face with their wings, their whole beings express their love and praise. Although there is no touch of envy in his tone, rather a great admiration and wonder, the poet states clearly that theirs is the best service. This superlative, I think, can refer only to the contrast between angels and men.

The exalted *Sanctus* at the end of the poem is ostensibly the angels' song of praise, an example of the optimum manner of glorifying God. In the Preface of the Mass, the angels, archangels, dominations, and powers are represented as singing the subsequent *Sanctus*, but we are expected to sing along with them (*Cum quibus et nostras voces. . . .*). The poet brings in his recurrent *ūs* as he has done in the closing petition of most of the poems, but he does it gradually and almost imperceptibly. As the angels' hymn progresses, it appears that God's *dōm* dwells *eorðlīc mid ældum*, a detail that would be more appropriate coming from the men themselves. His glory fills earth, as well as heaven, and the bright praise is also *in eorðan* and *mid beornum*. In the *Benedictus*, *dugeþum cwōme* suggests his coming to men (actually these words, along with lines 6 and 7, are the thin thread which connects this poem to the other Advent poems), but of course this may apply, like *weoroda* of line 30 and *wīgendra* of line 32, to either angels or men. Before the poem is over, the accumulation of these hints creates the impression that the hymn is coming from the mouths of both God's mortal and immortal worshippers. The poet, in bringing the angels and men together, thus provides a synthesis of the contrast presented in the earlier sections of the poem. Before it is finished, this lyric, in addition to being one of the most exalted and fervent of the series, becomes one of the most carefully constructed.

*POEM XII.* The antiphon which provides the poet with his springboard for this poem does indeed begin with *O*, but it is not one of the Advent *O*'s and was not sung at the *Magnificat*. It reflects some of the same ideas as the other antiphons since it was also used during the period after Christmas when the Church was rejoicing in the fact of the Incarnation. Perhaps the poet was attracted to this antiphon because he found here again the idea of the mysterious, spotless virgin birth

*INTRODUCTION*

which he always delighted to treat. After he dwells on that idea for a time, he departs completely from the antiphon and the manner of the poem from line 11 onward becomes that of incipient conclusion.

As in Poem xi the poet drops the structural pattern of the earlier lyrics and includes no petition, but he does bring in one or two of the themes which have run through his series, such as the difficulty for man to understand the secrets of God, and the help performed to men by the Grace of God. He then ends the poem with another joyous passage on the advisability for man to proffer praise and worship to God. The simplicity of the poem is what makes it a worthy conclusion for this series of lyrics; in almost essential form the final lines capture the characteristic attitude of the poet, visible in virtually every poem: his joy and hopefulness as he offers grateful praise for God's gift of Christ.

The entire series is a rather amazing production for ninth-century England. That there was a strong impulse among Old English writers to paraphrase and express in English some of the more beautiful of the Church's hymns and Psalms, we have ample evidence in the Paris Psalter and in the many fragments of poetic hymns, creeds, paternosters, and the like. These attempts, it is true, seldom rise above the pedestrian, and we almost never feel that a real poet is at work. In the Advent Lyrics, however, we are often aware that the Latin lyric form has found a worthy practitioner in English.

I hope it is clear from the critical comments on the individual poems that the poet's methods in writing the lyrics were many and various. In poems iii, iv and v he remained fairly close to his antiphonal source. In Poem vi, his adherence to the antiphon is close, but at the same time his expansions and shifts of emphasis produce a poem of real originality. Poems ii and ix show him diverging widely from the known antiphons, but carrying along their structural pattern, their tone, and some of their ideas. Poems x and xi show even greater independence and skill in fitting outside material into the poetic form he had chosen. Poem vii appears to be sheer poetic creation, where even the antiphonal structure is put aside and all the poetic tools are employed to draw fresh effects from the religious themes the poet so often treats during the series.

The antiphons of Advent are undeniably important to this series in many ways, but they are far from being the only sources. Woven throughout the poems in an all-pervasive manner is a consciousness of the whole liturgy, and for that matter, almost the whole Christian religion. Ideas from one antiphon creep into the poem based on another. Fragments of the creed or memories of Biblical story or echoes of the preface from the Mass appear sporadically. The emotions and ideas of the sources were so well assimilated into the poet's make-up that it is almost impossible to point to this, this, and this as the source for that line or that line or that line. In all probability the poet was a monk. He was accustomed to hearing the office and chanting the hours day after day, Advent after Advent. It had become a part of him, and its phrases as well as its concepts were part of his mind and his being. When he decided to write a poem dealing with the Advent, those phrases and concepts issued forth again, but only after having been filtered through his own imagination. Some of the poems he constructed were not at all effective, but on the other hand some of them were eminently successful from almost any point of view. In the best of the poems, and in the effect of the group as a whole, we are made vividly aware that we are here dealing with a genuine lyric sensitivity.

## Date and Dialect

SINCE THIS IS THE FIRST TIME the Advent Lyrics have been studied as a composition separate from the Cynewulf canon, we must approach the question of their date and locality of origin without any preconceptions. Cynewulf's poetry has long been considered, as indeed has most Old English poetry, to have been written in the Anglian dialect in a relatively early period and later copied by a series of West Saxon scribes. We must now scrutinize the evidence carefully, however, before we affirm that this sort of origin and transmission applies also to the Advent Lyrics. Virtually the only evidence we have is the internal linguistic testimony, since there are no historical references or other external clues to its history.

The date of the writing of the Exeter MS provides us with a *terminus ante quem* for the composition of the poem. This MS has long been dated rather vaguely at the end of the tenth century or the beginning of the eleventh, but Robin Flower, who made what is by far the most careful study of the handwriting of the MS, was inclined to localize the writing "in the West Country early in the period 970-990."[1] Even he, however, was wary of dating a MS on the basis of paleography alone, so that perhaps the old vagueness is inescapable. We can affirm with certainty only that our poems were written down in the Exeter Book shortly before the beginning of the eleventh century.

The language of the poem, like that of the MS as a whole, is predominantly West Saxon. At least ninety percent of the words offer no evidence to allow us to be more specific. Some few, of course, show characteristics which we associate with the late period of the Saxon dialect, but these are not especially

---

[1] Facsimile, p. 90. The abbreviations which follow in this chapter refer to the standard works on OE phonology and dialectology: L = Karl Luick, *Historische Grammatik der Englischen Sprache*, Leipzig, 1914-1929; B = Karl Bülbring, *Altenglisches Elementarbuch*, Heidelberg, 1902; S-B = Sievers-Brunner, *Altenglische Grammatik*, Halle, 1942. These works are cited by paragraph number.

numerous. Many words which would have been spelled with an *ie* (from various phonological sources) in the earlier period appear with a *y* in these poems: *scyppend, hȳrdon,* etc. In most cases, the old "*festes y*" remains, but in *flihte* XI 22, and *þrim* XII 8 (beside frequent *þrym*), we find the LWS characteristic of *y* appearing as *i* (L§ 281). In *-scypes* XII 19 and *fyrwet* IV 22, older *i* appears as *y*, also a later characteristic (L§ 285; S-B§ 22, a.2). In *wor(u)ld-* (4x) an earlier *eo* has changed to *o*, influenced by the preceding *w*, but this phonological development might be Northumbrian as well as LWS (S-B§ 113; L§ 222). These late factors, of course, prove very little except that at least one copyist was a West Saxon living sometime in the middle or late tenth century.

The following phonological phenomena might reveal more about possibly Anglian or Early West Saxon traces in the poems. With regard to the treatment of i-umlaut of *ēa*, we have: *nīedþīowa* X 13, *onlȳseð* III 19, *lȳfað* V 16, *ȳwe* VIII 32, *hȳneð* VIII 47, *dēgol* II 24, and possibly *genēdde* (MS *geneðde*) III 20. The *y* spellings, of course, are LWS, the *ie* is EWS (B§ 188) and the two *e*'s are apparently Anglian (S-B§ 104). However, *dēgol* appears in some WS prose manuscripts (B§ 317; S-B§ 106, a.1) and *genēdde* should not be used as evidence since it depends on emendation. With regard to the phenomenon known as palatalization, the treatment is thoroughly West Saxon: *-giefe* IV 10, *forgifnesse* XII 12, *forgildeð* XII 19, *gīet* IX 44, X 4, *ceaster* IX 40, *forgeaf* XI 14. The word *giofu* II 25 presents a problem in that the *io* cannot be ascribed to any OE dialect with any certainty.[2]

Breaking of *a* before *l* plus another consonant occurs in most words in the normal Saxon fashion: *healle* I 4, *ealdor* I 8, VIII 16, etc. An unbroken *a* occurs in *alwihte* VIII 61 and *waldend* (8x, counting other forms of the same root). This

[2] The Exeter scribe at one point wrote *geryno*, then later corrected it to *geryne* (IV 4), and at another wrote *brogo*, which he subsequently altered to *brego* (XI 26). Perhaps *giofu*, and possibly *hio* (IX 48), show similar, but uncorrected writings of *o* for *e*.

## INTRODUCTION

unbroken *a* is the normal Anglian development, but it also occurs fairly often in pure ews texts (L§ 146, a.2; S-B§ 85, a.1), so these forms can prove only that a lws origin is unlikely.

The diphthong *īo* (later *ēo*) under the conditions producing i-umlaut sometimes shows an umlauted vowel and sometimes does not: *inlīhted* II 26, *inlīhtes* v 5, *onlȳhte* VI 41 (but *inlēohte* v 12), *līxende* VIII 18, *þȳstro* VIII 14 (but *þēostrum* v 13). In general, the West Saxon dialect shows umlaut, whereas Anglian and Kentish do not (B§ 188, 191), but in ews the unumlauted *īo*'s and *ēo*'s also appear with some frequency (S-B§ 107). Forms of *-līht* are sometimes considered Anglian smoothed forms (S-B§ 119), but they also appear with *ī* in pure ws texts.

With regard to the combination *a* plus nasal, we find a very great majority of words spelled with *o*: *londes* XII 22, *wone* VIII 56, *somed* IV 21, etc. There are a few cases of *a*: *manna* IV 15, *gehwane* v 4, *lange* X 26, *onfangen* IV 29, *anginne* v 8. This phenomenon is a very unreliable criterion of dialect, since both vowels appear to some extent in all dialects, and arguments from relative proportions are extremely unconvincing. We would expect, however, many more *a* spellings if the poem originated in the late period in the Saxon area (B§ 123).

Velar umlaut of *a* may have occurred in the following words: *searocræft* I 9, *nearo-* III 20, *bealo-* VIII 46, *-ceare* VII 46, *geatu* VIII 38 (beside *gatu* IX 45). As a rule, *a* does not undergo umlaut in these words in ws (B§ 232), although Sievers-Brunner point out that it does appear sporadically in some texts (§ 109 a.1). Furthermore, several of the forms, like *ceare* and *geatu*, might be explained as having analogical diphthongs from other cases where palatalization would occur (L§ 231, a.2). Velar umlaut of *i* occurs in *cleopast* VII 14, *leofa* XI 35, *leomo* I 15, *lioðu-* IX 61. In the first two words umlaut occurs in all dialects of oe (L§ 224, S-B§ 111), but

{ 38 }

in the last two, before a dental or nasal consonant, it is not common in West Saxon. Even here, however, we do not have a clear-cut testimony against Saxon authorship, for umlauted forms do sometimes occur (L§ 224 a.1; S-B§ 111 a.2). The numerous *io* spellings, from this and from other sources, which we see in *lioðu*, *þiowa*, *iowa*, *sio*, etc., would be normal enough in either EWS or Northumbrian, but unusual in LWS or Mercian (S-B§ 78). *e* undergoes velar umlaut in every occurrence of the word *meotud* (7x), which is not normal in WS (L§ 228; S-B§ 110), but naturally since this word was part of the poetic vocabulary, it could have been taken over, phonology and all, in its Anglian form even if the poem were written by a Saxon.

There are some forms in the poems, however, which do seem to be distinctively and inescapably Anglian. Smoothed vowels occur in *gereht* VI 4 (B§ 209) and *geslæhte* VI 20 (B§ 205). *gereht*, it might be argued, could also be LWS, since it sometimes occurs in Aelfric (B§ 313), but I find no indication that *geslæhte* occurs outside Anglian texts. Also, with regard to the treatment of i-umlaut of *a* under breaking conditions, we find (beside many cases, of course, showing LWS phonology): *ældum* XI 29, *gehþum* IV 20, *elda* IX 37, *wærgða* IV 28, *wærgðo* III 8, *ermðu* VIII 58 (but *yrmða* X 23) and possibly *ælmihtig-* (5x). These forms are typically Anglian (B§ 175, 176, 180; L§ 188, 194).

I have most often used the term Anglian in the discussion above for convenience, for in most cases distinctions between Mercian and Northumbrian cannot be made. As I have pointed out, there are two phenomena which might indicate Northumbrian provenience, and to them we might add *geondsprēot* II 25, which would normally appear as *geondsprēat* in WS and Mercian. *eo*'s instead of *ea*'s are common in the (southern?) Northumbrian dialect of Rushworth 2 (L§ 119, 127; B§ 140). Even if this *eo* does not reflect a momentary scribal lapse, it could be ascribed, along with the few other Northumbrian forms,[3] to a Northumbrian copyist somewhere in the intermediate transmission as easily as to the author himself.

Turning to other sorts of evidence, we find no syncope of the ending in the second and third persons singular, present tense of strong verbs: *bideð* v 10, *spricest* vii 16, *spriceð* ii 16, *onlūceð* ix 51, *healdeð* ii 2, *ābūgeð* ii 7, *ontȳneð* ii 2, *gesēceð* iii 13, etc. In most cases these long forms are required by the meter, and must have been used by the poet himself in composing the verse. This phenomenon, as Sievers demonstrated,[4] is a relatively good indication of Anglian provenience. If long forms were accepted into the poetic tradition, of course, they might also appear in poems by Saxon poets, as indeed they do here and there in the Meters of Boethius. It must be admitted, however, that in none of the surely Saxon poems do we find such consistent and exclusive use of long forms as we find in the Advent Lyrics.

The form *heht* ix 20 is often considered Anglian or poetic, or both, but it occasionally appears in Alfredian Texts. The preterite singular of the verb *onwrēon* appears six times as *onwrāh* in these poems, and this is the normal form in the Anglian dialects. In ws this verb sometimes, though not always, took the form *onwrēah* by analogy with verbs of class ii (S-B§ 383). The past participle *gesewen* v 22 occurs in its Saxon form rather than its Anglian equivalent *gesegen* (S-B § 234, a.2; § 391, a.8).

When we consider the vocabulary of the poem with the idea of dialect in mind, we find the following well-known Anglian words:[5] *bealu* vii 19 (and compounds), *gēn* vii 29,

---

[3] The infinitive *inhebba* (ix 39) should be mentioned here in order to be absolutely fair, although I think it very unlikely that it is a bona fide Northumbrian form. A nasal macron over the *a* of a more southern infinitive form could very easily have been lost in transmission.

[4] *Beiträge zur Geschichte der deutschen Sprache und Literatur*, 10, pp. 464ff.

[5] The most important studies of dialect vocabulary are those of Richard Jordan, *Eigentümlichkeiten des Anglischen Wortschatzes*, Heidelberg, 1906, and Günther Scherer, *Zur Geographie und Chronologie des angelsächsischen*

35 (beside *gīet* IX 45) *herenis* XI 38, *līxan* VIII 18, *morþor* VII 30, *nymðe* IX 51 (beside *būtan* VIII 59), *weorc*⁶ III 18, *worn* VII 6. Of course, all of these words occur repeatedly in many poems, and it might be claimed that the poet used them as poeticisms. Yet a Saxon poet used his own normal dialect as well as the conventionalized poetic diction in writing his poems, and it would be highly unusual for him to write a poem without any distinctive Saxonisms. Of the two thousand odd words in these poems, I have discovered no word which is peculiar to the Saxon dialect. There are two words, *nǣnig* II 22, IX 50 and *carcern* II 8, which militate against the poem's original composition in LWS.⁷

The linguistic evidence presented above is, to my mind, extremely inconclusive. Several years ago Mr. Kenneth Sisam wrote an essay⁸ on the dialect origins of OE poetry in which, although he proved almost nothing, he raised plausible doubts as to the validity of the conventional facile ascription of texts to the North. It is particularly important that we be wary in a case like the present one, where only linguistic evidence is available. Most of the phonological phenomena discussed above would fit an Early West Saxon poet, well schooled in the earlier tradition, as well as an Anglian one. Forms like *gīet*, *nīed-*, and *-giefe* make it clear that there was at least an Early West Saxon stage in the copying of the poem. The list of inescapably Anglian forms is relatively small, and conceivably could have been introduced by a Mercian scribe copy-

---

*Wortschatzes*, Berlin, 1928. The words in the list following are discussed in one or the other of these books.

⁶ This word I take as the Anglian *wærc* (See Jordan, *Eigentümlichkeiten*, p. 51). I suspect, furthermore, that all the words listed in Bosworth-Toller under *weorc* VII, and in Grein's *Sprachschatz* under *weorce* are simply cases where Saxon scribes mistakenly adapted a strange dialectal word to a form more familiar to them, but unfortunately the form they took to be cognate had a different meaning, and was in fact a different word.

⁷ See K. T. Jost, *Wulfstanstudien*, Bern, 1950, pp. 159ff. and R. J. Menner, *Philologica: The Malone Anniversary Studies*, Baltimore, 1949, p. 59.

⁸ "Dialect Origins of the Earlier Old English Verse," *Studies in the History of Old English Literature*, Oxford, 1953.

*INTRODUCTION*

ing the poem sometime during the tenth century. With the matter thus in balance, the scale is tipped, I think, by the rather large number of Anglian words, plus the exclusive use of the long forms of the second and third persons singular of the present tense of strong verbs. We would be forced to postulate an unnaturally meticulous and imitative poet if we assumed Saxon authorship. All things considered, I think the poet was most likely a Mercian, and that his poem was copied by at least one Early West Saxon scribe and one Late West Saxon. In all probability there were other copyists in between.

As to the date, I must be equally general. When dealing with the Anglian dialects, we have few or no tests for judging early and late. There are at least no extremely early features, such as we find in the early glossaries of the seventh and eighth centuries. The Cynewulfian poetry is most often placed in the late eighth or early ninth century, but I see no reason why the Advent Lyrics could not just as well have been written in the late ninth century. There are a few factors, such as the *ie* spellings, which indicate a date around the Alfredian period, but no linguistic features in the text suggest a period earlier than that.

In the treatment of the unaccented syllables, we often find evidence of Late Old English developments. *worde* for *worda* VII 6, *læmena* for *læmenu* I 15, *stōdan* for *stōdon* VIII 39, *eardedon* for *eardodon* V 22, and possibly *hetlen* X 17 and *inlocast* XII 17 show orthographic substitutions due to late phonetic weakening of unaccented syllables.[9] This phenomenon is also common throughout the other poems in the Exeter Book; it can prove only the relatively late date of the MS and tells us nothing about the time the poems were written.

---

[9] The list could easily be extended: *usse* for *ussa* VIII 48, *wærgða* for *wærgðu* IV 28, *mōtan* for *mōton* VIII 33, XI 15, *hyhtan* for *hyhton* VI 13, *stondeð* for *stondað* IX 48, etc. Although this phenomenon is well-known, I have emended a few of these forms where I thought the clarity of the text would benefit. Perhaps the form *mæra* IX 1, where we would expect *mære*, is a back formation produced by this phonetic and orthographic confusion.

the Lyrics

## note on the translation

THE modern English of this translation is always, I hope, intelligible, but it will often seem bizarre and novel in construction. I have attempted to stay close to the Old English (sometimes proceeding line by line) in order to give some flavor of the Old English phrase order and idiom and also to facilitate reference to the original text. In matters of rendering the exact connotations of many words or the precise nuance of some constructions, I have often had to admit failure, as does any translator of poetry. No translation, with its necessary simplifications and compromises, is a substitute for the poem in the original language, but it is hoped that this one, when used with the glossary and the notes, will aid those readers whose Old English is rusty to get closer to the original poems.

## note on the text

THE text is based on a first hand transcript on the MS. The ultraviolet photographs made for the Facsimile edition have also been of great value, some of their readings being registered in that edition and some later by K-D and Ker (*Medium Aevum* II, 224-231). I have also consulted, without much profit, the copy of the MS made by Robert Chambers in 1836 (B.M. Additional MS 9067).

I have collated all the previous editions, but have decided not to publish all the variants. Cook's edition has all the variants up to his time, and the only later complete text is that of K-D, with whose text mine agrees except for punctuation and a few readings discussed in the notes. Many of the conjectures of the earlier editors about the illegible passages have no value and very little interest since the ultraviolet prints have revealed reliable readings.

In printing the text, I have put in italics anything that has not been verified in the MS. The exact MS reading in each case can be seen at the bottom of the page, and any emendations or additions which are not obvious scribal miswritings are explained in the notes. Common abbreviations (7, ƀ, scā, ę, and the nasal macron) have been tacitly expanded.

# I

.... to the King.
You are the wall-stone which the workmen of old
rejected from the work. Indeed it is fitting
that you be the head of the great hall,
and draw together the vast walls,
the unbroken flint, with a firm joining,
in order that throughout earth's cities all things
    with the gift of sight
may wonder eternally, O Lord of Glory.
Reveal now by your mysterious skill your own work,
O true and victorious One, and then leave standing
wall against wall. Now for your works there is need
that the Maker come, the King himself,
and thereupon repair—it is now decayed—
the house under its roof. He created the body,
the limbs of clay. Now must the Lord
save this weary multitude from wrath,
the wretched ones from terror, as He has often done.

# I

*O Rex gentium et desideratus earum, lapisque angularis qui facis utraque unum: veni, et salva hominem quem de limo formasti.*

                    . . . . cyninge.

Ðu eart se weallstan      þe ða wyrhtan iu
wiðwurpon to weorce.     Wel þe geriseð
þæt þu heafod sie       healle mærre
ond gesomnige      side weallas                   5
fæste gefoge,       flint unbræcne,
þæt geond eorðbyrg eall     eagna gesihþe
wundrien to worlde     wuldres ealdor.
Gesweotula nu þurh searocræft     þin sylfes weorc,
soðfæst, sigorbeorht,     ond sona forlæt          10
weall wið wealle.     Nu is þam weorce þearf
þæt se cræftga cume     ond se cyning sylfa,
ond þonne gebete—     nu gebrosnad is—
hus under hrofe.     He þæt hra gescop,
leomo læmena.     Nu sceal liffrea             15
þone wergan heap     wraþum ahreddan,
earme from egsan,     swa he oft dyde.

4 *heafoð*      7 *eorðb::g*      12 *cræstga*

## II

You, O Lord and true King,
who govern the locks, you open and reveal Life.
The exalted paths to another you deny,
the glorious journey, if his acts are not worthy.
We, indeed of necessity, speak these words
and . . . . . . . . . . he who created man
that he not . . . . . . . . . . . .
the affairs of the miserable, those who in prison
sit sorrowing. We yearn for the sun,
when the Lord of Life may release the light,
may be to our spirits as a strengthener
and envelop in magnificence our faltering minds,
may make us worthy that he has admitted us to glory,
those who miserably had to turn
to this narrow world, deprived of homeland.
One may say—he who speaks truth—
that He rescued, when it was lost,
the race of men. The girl was young,
a virgin free of sin, she whom He chose for a mother.
It was accomplished without the love of a man
that the bride was magnified by the birth of a child.
Nothing approaching that, before or since,
no such merit of woman existed in the world.
Such a thing is miraculous, a mystery of God.
All spiritual gifts sprang up throughout the earth;
then many a shoot became illumined
by the Giver of Life, old knowledge
which formerly in dark soil lay planted,
the chants of the prophets, when the Ruler came,
he who enlarges the secret meaning of each speech
of those who fittingly, in a wise way,
will praise the name of the Creator.

## II

*O clavis David, et sceptrum domus Israel, qui aperis et nemo claudit; claudis et nemo aperit: veni et educ vinctum de domo carceris, sedentem in tenebris et umbra mortis.*

Eala þu reccend     ond þu riht cyning,
se þe locan healdeð,     lif ontyneð,
eadgan upwegas,     oþrum forwyrneð
wlitigan wilsiþes,     gif his weorc ne deag.
Huru we for þearfe     þas word sprecað     5
ond m:::giað     þone þe mon gescop
þæt he ne :ete::: ceose weorðan
cearfulra þing,     þe we in carcerne
sittað sorgende.     Sunnan wenað,
hwonne us liffrea     leoht ontyne,     10
weorðe ussum mode     to mundboran,
ond þæt tydre gewitt     tire bewinde,
gedo usic þæs wyrðe     þe he to wuldre forlet
þa þe heanlice     hweorfan sceoldan
to þis enge lond,     eðle bescyrede.     15
Forþon secgan mæg,     se ðe soð spriceð,
þæt he ahredde,     þa forhwyrfed wæs,
frumcyn fira.     Wæs seo fæmne geong,
mægð manes leas,     þe he him to meder geceas.
Þæt wæs geworden     butan weres frigum     20
þæt þurh bearnes gebyrd     bryd eacen wearð.
Nænig efenlic þam,     ær ne siþþan,
in worlde gewearð     wifes gearnung;
þæt degol wæs,     dryhtnes geryne.
Eal giofu gæstlic     grundsceat geondspreot;     25
þær wisna fela     wearð inlihted
lare longsume     þurh lifes fruman
þe ær under hoðman     biholen lægon,
witgena woðsong,     þa se waldend cwom,
se þe reorda gehwæs     ryne gemiclað     30
ðara þe geneahhe     noman scyppendes
þurh horscne had     hergan willað.

1 *Eala þa*     3 *eadga*     32 *hosc ne*

# III

O vision of peace, holy Jerusalem,
best of royal thrones, homeland of Christ,
native seat of angels, where those alone,
the souls of the steadfast, always dwell
exultant in glory. Never a touch of vileness
in that region is ever seen,
rather every crime is exiled far from you,
every evil and struggle. You are gloriously full
of holy joy, as your name promises.
Look yourself now, that through the wide creation
you may broadly survey, the roof of heaven also
on every side, how Heaven's King
seeks you widely and Himself comes.
He makes his home in you, as long ago
wise prophets predicted;
they proclaimed Christ's birth, they spoke
    comfort to you,
brightest of cities. Now has that man come,
been born to mitigate the pain of the Hebrews;
He brings joy to you, He loosens the chains
imposed by sin. He knows the dire need,
that the wretched must await grace.

## III

*O Hierusalem, civitas Dei summi: leva in circuitu oculos tuos, et vide Dominum tuum, quia jam veniet solvere te a vinculis.*

Eala sibbe gesihð,    sancta hierusalem,
cynestola cyst,    cristes burglond,
engla eþelstol,    ond þa ane in þe
saule soðfæstra    simle gerestað,
wuldrum hremge.    Næfre wommes tacn    5
in þam eardgearde    eawed weorþeð,
ac þe firena gehwylc    feor abugeð,
wærgðo ond gewinnes.    Bist to wuldre full
halgan hyhtes,    swa þu gehaten eart.
Sioh nu sylfa,    þe geond þas sidan gesceaft,    10
swylce rodores hrof    rume geondwlit*e*
ymb healfa gehwone,    hu þec heofones cyning
siðe geseceð,    ond sylf cymeð.
Nimeð eard in þe,    swa hit ær gefyrn
witgan wisfæste    wordum sægdon;    15
cyðdon cristes gebyrd,    cwædon þe to frofre,
burga betlicast.    Nu is þæt bearn cymen,
awæcned to wyrpe    weorcum ebrea,
bringeð blisse þe,    benda onlyseð,
niþum gene*d*de.    Nearoþearfe conn,    20
hu se earma sceal    are gebidan.

11 *geondwlitan*    15 *worðum* corrected to *wordum*    20 *geneðde*

## IV

"O joy of women, beyond all glories
noblest woman in all the earth
of whom mortals have heard tell,
explain to us the mystery that came to you from the skies,
how you ever received a magnification
by the birth of a child, and intercourse
according to human notions never knew.
We truly have not heard of such a thing
ever happening in earlier days,
that which you received in such special grace,
nor have we reason to expect that event
in time to come. Indeed truth in you
dwelt worthy, when you the power of heaven
bore in your womb, yet was not fouled
your great virginity. As all the children of men
sow in sorrow, so reap they again,
give birth for death." The Blessed Virgin spoke,
forever filled with triumph, Holy Mary:
"What is this wonderment whereby you marvel,
and sorrowing lament in grief,
son of Salem and his daughter?
For curiosity do you ask how I the state of virginity,
my purity, maintained, and also became the exalted mother
of the Son of God? That, however, to men is not
an open secret, but Christ did reveal
in the dear kinswoman of David
that the sin of Eve is all nullified,
the curse overthrown, and the lowlier sex
is made great. Now hope is received
that blessing may rest with both together,
with men and women always henceforth
in the exalted joy of the angels
with the True Father forever, world without end."

## IV

*O virgo virginum, quomodo fiet istud, quia nec primam similem visa es nec habere sequentem? Filiae Jerusalem, quid me admiramini? Divinum est mysterium hoc quod cernitis.*

"Eala wifa wynn,     geond wuldres þrym
fæmne freolicast     ofer ealne foldan sceat
þæs þe æfre sundbuend     secgan hyrdon,
arece us þæt geryne     þæt þe of roderum cwom,
hu þu eacnunge     æfre onfenge     5
bearnes þurh gebyrde     ond þone gebedscipe
æfter monwisan     mod ne cuðes.
Ne we soðlice     swylc ne gefrugnan
in ærdagum     æfre gelimpan
þæt ðu in sundurgiefe     swylce befenge,     10
ne we þære wyrde     wenan þurfon
toweard in tide.     Huru treow in þe
weorðlicu wunade,     nu þu wuldres þrym
bosme gebære,     ond no gebrosnad wearð
mægðhad se micla.     Swa eal manna bearn     15
sorgum sawað,     swa eft ripað,
cennað to cwealme."     Cwæð sio eadge mæg
symle sigores full,     sancta maria:
"Hwæt is þeos wundrung     þe ge wafiað
ond geomrende     gehþum mænað,     20
sunu solimæ     somod his dohtor?
Fricgað þurh fyrwet     hu ic fæmnan had,
mund minne geheold,     ond eac modor gewearð
mære meotudes suna?     Forþan þæt monnum nis
cuð geryne,     ac crist onwrah     25
in dauides     dyrre mægan
þæt is euan scyld     eal forpynded,
wærgða aworpen,     ond gewuldrad is
se heanra had.     Hyht is onfangen
þæt nu bletsung mot     bæm gemæne,     30
werum ond wifum,     a to worulde forð
in þam uplican     engla dreame
mid soðfæder     symle wunian."

4 **geryne** final *e* corrected from *o*

## V

O Radiance, brightest of angels
sent to men throughout the earth
and veritable splendor of the sun,
dazzling beyond the stars, you ever enlighten
of your self every era of time.
Since you, God of God, begotten of old,
son of the True Father in the glory of heaven
without beginning always existed,
so now your own works in dire need
ask confidently that you send us
the bright sun, and come yourself
that you may illumine those who long before,
covered with darkness and obscurity here,
have sat in continual night; enshrouded in sin
we had to endure the dark shadow of death.
Now we hopefully believe in the salvation
brought to men by the word of God,
which was at the beginning coeternal
with God, the Father Almighty, and now has become
flesh free from stain which the virgin bore
as a help to the miserable. God was among us
seen without sin; together they lived,
mighty son of God and son of man
in harmony among people. For that we may
utter thanks forever to the Lord for his acts,
for he willed to send himself to us.

## V

*O Oriens, splendor lucis aeternae et sol justitiae: veni et illumina sedentem in tenebris et umbra mortis.*

Eala earendel,    engla beorhtast,
ofer middangeard    monnum sended,
ond soðfæsta    sunnan leoma,
torht ofer tunglas,    þu tida gehwane
of sylfum þe    symle inlihtes.    5
Swa þu, god of gode    gearo acenned,
sunu soþan fæder,    swegles in wuldre
butan anginne    æfre wære,
swa þec nu for þearfum    þin agen geweorc
bideð þurh byldo    þæt þu þa beorhtan us    10
sunnan onsende,    ond þe sylf cyme
þæt ðu inleohte    þa þe longe ær,
þrosme beþeahte    ond in þeostrum her,
sæton sinneahtes;    synnum bifealdne
deorc deaþes sceadu    dreogan sceoldan.    15
Nu we hyhtfulle    hælo gelyfað
þurh þæt word godes    weorodum brungen,
þe on frymðe wæs    fæder ælmihtigum
efenece mid god,    ond nu eft gewearð
flæsc firena leas    þæt seo fæmne gebær    20
geomrun to geoce.    God wæs mid us
gesewen butan synnum;    somod eardedon
mihtig meotudes bearn    ond se monnes sunu
geþwære on þeode.    We þæs þonc magon
secgan sigedryhtne    symle bi gewyrhtum    25
þæs þe he hine sylfne us    sendan wolde.

10 *hyldo* corrected to *byldo*    15 *sceaðu* partially corrected to *sceadu*

## VI

O God of Spirits, how wisely you
were justly called by the name
Emmanuel, as the angel spoke it
first in Hebrew. That is interpreted
broadly by the meaning: "Now is the Guardian of the
 Heavens,
God Himself, with us." As prophets of old
said truly the King of all kings and also
the spotless priest was to come,
so of old the great Melchisedech,
wise in spirit, revealed the divine power
of the eternal Ruler. He was the Bringer of Law,
the Guide of Wisdom to those who long
had wished for his coming, as was promised to them,
that the son of God Himself would
cleanse the people of earth,
and also with a journey by the might of his spirit
visit the depths. For that they patiently
awaited in chains the time when the Son of God
should come to the wretched. They then spoke thus,
weakened by torment: "Now come yourself,
High King of Heaven. Bring the life of salvation to us,
to the weary prisoners overcome with crying,
with bitter salt tears. The remedy is completely
yours alone . . . . . . . . . . . . . .
heart-saddened captives hither . . . . .
Nor leave behind you when you turn hence
this great crowd, but your mercy upon us
make known royally, Savior Christ,
Prince of Heaven, nor let the cursed one over us
wield power. Leave us the eternal joy
of your glory that we may praise you,
Glory-King of people whom you long ago made
with your hands. In the highest
you live eternally with the Ruling Father."

## VI

*O Emmanuel, Rex et Legifer noster, exspectatio gentium et
salvator earum: veni ad salvandum nos, Dominus Deus noster.*

Eala gæsta god,     hu þu gleawlice
mid noman ryhte     nemned wære
emmanuhel,     swa hit engel gecwæð
ærest on ebresc!     Þæt is eft gereht,
rume bi gerynum:     "Nu is rodera weard,     5
god sylfa mid us."     Swa þæt gomele gefyrn
ealra cyninga cyning     ond þone clænan eac
sacerd soðlice     sægdon toweard;
swa se mæra iu,     melchisedech,
gleaw in gæste     godþrym onwrah     10
eces alwaldan.     Se wæs æ bringend,
lara lædend,     þam longe his
hyhtan hidercyme,     swa him gehaten wæs,
þætte sunu meotudes     sylfa wolde
gefælsian     foldan mægðe,     15
swylce grundas eac     gæstes mægne
siþe gesecan.     Nu hie softe þæs
bidon in bendum     hwonne bearn godes
cwome to cearigum.     Forþon cwædon swa,
suslum geslæhte:     "Nu þu sylfa cum,     20
heofones heahcyning.     Bring us hælo lif,
werigum witeþeowum,     wope forcymenum,
bitrum brynetearum.     Is seo bot gelong
eal æt þe anum     ::::::::oferþearfum.
Hæftas hygegeomre     hider ::::::es,     25
ne læt þe behindan,     þonne þu heonan cyrre,
mænigo þus micle,     ac þu miltse on us
gecyð cynelice,     crist nergende,
wuldres æþeling,     ne læt awyrgde ofer us
onwald agan.     Læf us ecne gefean     30
wuldres þines,     þæt þec weorðien,
weoroda wuldorcyning,     þa þu geworhtes ær
hondum þinum.     Þu in heannissum
wunast wideferh     mid waldend fæder."

4 *est*     8 *towearð* corrected to *toweard*

## VII

"O my Joseph, son of Jacob,
descendant of David the great king,
now must you sever a firm affection,
reject my love?" "I suddenly am
deeply disturbed, despoiled of honor,
for I have for you heard many words,
many great sorrows and hurtful speeches,
much harm, and to me they speak insult,
many hostile words. Tears I must
shed, sad in mind. God easily may
relieve the inner pain of my heart,
comfort the wretched one. O young girl,
Mary the virgin!" "What are you bewailing,
crying out full of care? Never did I guilt in you,
any fault ever find
of accomplished wrong, yet you speak these words
as if you yourself of every sin,
of crimes were filled." "I have too much
of evil received for this pregnancy.
How may I refute the hateful talk
or find any answer
against my enemies? It is widely known
that I from the bright temple of God
willingly received a pure virgin
free from stain, and now she is changed
by I know not what. It does me no good
either speaking or keeping silent. If I tell the truth,
then shall David's daughter die,
killed with stones. Yet it is worse
that I conceal the crime; a perjured man,
hateful to all people, would live hereafter
vile among the folk." Then the girl revealed
the true mystery, and spoke thus:
"The truth I utter through the Son of God,
Savior of Spirits, that I still do not know
by copulation any man,

## VII

"Eala ioseph min, iacobes bearn,
mæg dauides, mæran cyninges,
nu þu freode scealt fæste gedælan,
alætan lufan mine?" "Ic lungre eam
deope gedrefed, dome bereafod, 5
forðon ic worn for þe word*a* hæbbe
sidra sorga ond sarcwida,
hearmes gehyred, ond me hosp sprecað,
tornworda fela. Ic tearas sceal
geotan geomormod. God eaþe mæg 10
gehælan hygesorge heortan minre,
afrefran feasceaftne. Eala fæmne geong,
mægð maria!" "Hwæt bemurnest ðu,
cleopast cearigende? Ne ic culpan in þe,
incan ænigne, æfre onfunde, 15
womma geworhtra, ond þu þa word spricest
swa þu sylfa sie synna gehwylcre
firena gefylled." "Ic to fela hæbbe
þæs byrdscypes bealwa onfongen.
Hu mæg ic ladigan laþan spræce 20
oþþe ondsware ænige findan
wraþum towiþere? Is þæt wide cuð
þæt ic of þam torhtan temple dryhtnes
onfeng freolice fæmnan clæne,
womma lease, ond nu gehwyrfed is 25
þurh nathwylces. Me nawþer deag
secge ne swige. Gif ic soð sprece,
þonne sceal dauides dohtor sweltan,
stanum astyrfed. Gen strengre is
þæt ic morþor hele; scyle manswara, 30
laþ leoda gehwam lifgan siþþan,
fracoð in folcum." Þa seo fæmne onwrah
ryhtgeryno, ond þus reordade:
"Soð ic secge þurh sunu meotodes,
gæsta geocend, þæt ic gen ne conn 35
þurh gemæcscipe monnes ower,

any on earth, but to me it was granted,
young in my home, that Gabriel,
archangel of heaven, offered me a greeting.
He said truly that the Spirit of Heaven
would illumine me with splendor; I should bear the Glory
    of Life,
the bright Son, the mighty Child of God,
of the glorious Creator. Now that I his temple am
made without spot, in me the Spirit of Comfort
has dwelt, so you now may completely relinquish
your bitter sorrow. Say eternal thanks
to the great Son of God that I have become his mother,
yet henceforth a virgin, and you called his father
by the reckoning of the world. Prophecy had to be
in Himself truly fulfilled."

ænges on eorðan,    ac me eaden wearð,
geongre in geardum,    þæt me gabrihel,
heofones heagengel,    hælo gebodade.
Sægde soðlice    þæt me swegles gæst    40
leoman onlyhte,    sceolde ic lifes þrym
geberan, beorhtne sunu,    bearn eacen godes,
torhtes tirfruma*n*.    Nu ic his tempel eam
gefremed butan facne,    in me frofre gæst
geeardode,    nu þu ealle forlæt    45
sare sorgceare.    Saga ecne þonc
mærum meotodes sunu    þæt ic his modor gewearð,
fæmne forð seþeah,    ond þu fæder cweden
woruldcund bi wene.    Sceolde witedom
in him sylfum beon    soðe gefylled."

6 *worde*    43 *tirfruma*

## VIII

O true and pacific
King of all kings, Almighty Christ,
you existed before all
the glories of the world, by your wondrous Father
begotten a child by his power and might!
There is not now any man under the skies,
any clever-thinking man so deeply wise
that he may to mortals say,
explain aright how the Guardian of the Heavens
at the beginning took you as his noble Son.
Of the things which human kind
have heard among people, first
was effected under the skies that the Wise God,
Creator of Life, light and darkness
nobly separated, and his was the power of decision,
and he, Lord of Hosts, ordained the matter:
"Now let there be made henceforth always and eternally
light, shining joy to all the living
who in generations may come to be born."
Immediately it happened, when it had to be so;
brilliance enlightened the tribes of people,
bright among the stars, after the passage of time.
He Himself ordained that you his Son be
coeternal with your sole Lord
before any of this ever came about.
You are the Wisdom which shaped fully
this wide creation with the Ruling Father.
Therefore is there none so intelligent nor so clever
that he may to the children of men your parentage
clearly verify. Come now, Guard of Victory,
Lord of Mankind, and your mercy here,
Gracious One, show. For us all there is a yearning
that we your maternal kin may know
in truth, since we may not reckon
your paternal kin one whit further.

# VIII

*O Rex pacifice, tu ante saecula nate, per auream egredere portam: redemptos tuos visita, et eos illuc revoca unde ruerunt per culpam.*

Eala þu soða     ond þu sibsuma
ealra cyninga cyning,     crist ælmihtig,
hu þu ær wære     eallum geworden
worulde þrymmum     mid þinne wuldorfæder
cild acenned     þurh his cræft ond meaht!     5
Nis ænig nu     eorl under lyfte,
secg searoþoncol,     to þæs swiðe gleaw
þe þæt asecgan mæge     sundbuendum,
areccan mid ryhte     hu þe rodera weard
æt frymðe genom     him to freobearne.     10
Þæt wæs þara þinga     þe her þeoda cynn
gefrugnen mid folcum     æt fruman ærest
geworden under wolcnum,     þæt witig god,
lifes ordfruma,     leoht ond þystro
gedælde dryhtlice,     ond him wæs domes geweald,     15
ond þa wisan abead     weoroda ealdor:
"Nu sie geworden forþ     a to widan feore
leoht, lixende gefea,     lifgendra gehwam
þe in cneorissum     cende weorðen."
Ond þa sona gelomp,     þa hit swa sceolde,     20
leoma leohtade     leoda mægþum,
torht mid tunglum,     æfterþon tida bigong.
Sylfa sette     þæt þu sunu wære
efeneardigende     mid þinne engan frean
ærþon oht þisses     æfre gewurde.     25
Þu eart seo snyttro     þe þas sidan gesceaft
mid þi waldende     worhtes ealle.
Forþon nis ænig þæs horsc,     ne þæs hygecræftig
þe þin fromcyn mæge     fira bearnum
sweotule geseþan.     Cum nu, sigores weard,     30
meotod moncynnes,     ond þine miltse her
arfæst ywe.     Us is eallum neod
þæt we þin medrencynn     motan cunnan,
ryhtgeryno,     nu we areccan ne mægon
þæt fædrencynn     fier owihte.     35

Mildly bless this middle world
with your advent, Savior Christ,
and those golden gates, which in former days
a long while ago stood locked,
command to be opened, O High Lord of Heaven,
and then seek us by your visit,
humble on earth. We need your grace.
The accursed wolf, beast of dark deeds,
has scattered your flock, Lord,
widely dispersed it; that which you earlier, God,
bought with blood, the evil one
oppresses bitterly and takes for himself into captivity
against our desires. Therefore we, Savior,
pray you eagerly in our heartfelt thoughts
that you quickly extend help
to the weary exiles, that the torturing killer
into hell's depths miserable may fall,
and your handiwork, Creator of Men,
may arise and come aright
to the heavenly, noble kingdom
whence the dark spirit formerly through sin-lust
pulled and ensnared us, so that we, stripped of glory,
ever without end must endure privation
unless you more quickly, Eternal Lord,
Living God, Guardian of all beings,
will save us from the injurer.

Þu þisne middangeard  milde geblissa
þurh ðinne hercyme,  hælende crist,
ond þa gyldnan geatu,  þe in geardagum
ful longe ær  bilocen stodan,
heofona heahfrea,  hat ontynan, 40
ond usic þonne gesece  þurh þin sylfes gong
eaðmod to eorðan.  Us is þinra arna þearf!
Hafað se awyrgda  wulf tostenced,
deor dædscua*n*,  dryhten, þin eowde,
wide towrecene,  þæt ðu, waldend, ær 45
blode gebohtes,  þæt se bealofulla
hyneð heardlice,  ond him on hæft nimeð
ofer usse nioda lust.  Forþon we, nergend, þe
biddað geornlice  breostgehygdum
þæt þu hrædlice  helpe gefremme 50
wergum wreccan,  þæt se wites bona
in helle grund  hean gedreose,
ond þin hondgeweorc,  hæleþa scyppend,
mote arisan  ond on ryht cuman
to þam upcundan  æþelan rice, 55
þonan us ær þurh synlust  se swearta gæst
forteah ond fortylde,  þæt we, tires wone,
a butan ende  sculon ermþu dreogan,
butan þu usic þon ofostlicor,  ece dryhten,
æt þam leodsceaþan,  lifgende god, 60
helm alwihta,  hreddan wille.

12 *gefrugnen* altered from *gefrunen*  31 *milstse*
44 *dædscua*  44 *eowde* corrected from *eowðe*

{ 65 }

# IX

O Great One of the world,
throughout the earth the purest lady
of those who have existed ever,
how rightly all possessors of speech,
men upon earth, name you and say
with glad heart that you are the bride
of the most excellent Lord of the sky.
Also the highest in heaven,
Christ's nobles, speak and sing
that you by holy power are the lady
of the heavenly host as well as the earthly
ranks under the heavens and the inhabitants of hell.
You, alone among all mankind
resolved splendidly, firm-minded,
that you brought your virginity to God,
gave it without sin. None like that came,
no other from all humanity,
no crowned bride who the bright gift
with spotless spirit to our heaven-home
has sent. For that the Lord of Victory commanded
his high messenger to fly hither
from his glorious majesty and reveal quickly to you
the fullness of power, that you the Son of God
might bear in a pure birth
as a mercy to men, and henceforth might keep
yourself, Mary, ever immaculate.
We also have heard that long ago about you
a certain true prophet, Isaiah,
said in the days long past
that he was led where he could view
the whole arena of life in that heavenly home.

# IX

*O mundi Domina, regio ex semine orta, ex tuo jam Christus processit alvo, tanquam sponsus de thalamo; hic jacet in praesepio qui et sidera regit.*

Eala þu mæra        middangeardes
seo clæneste        cwen ofer eorþan
þara þe gewurde        to widan feore,
hu þec mid ryhte        ealle reordberend
hatað ond secgað,        hæleð geond foldan,      5
bliþe mode,        þæt þu bryd sie
þæs selestan        swegles bryttan.
Swylce þa hyhstan        on heofonum eac,
cristes þegnas,        cweþað ond singað
þæt þu sie hlæfdige        halgum meahtum      10
wuldorweorudes,        ond worldcundra
hada under heofonum        ond helwara.
Forþon þu þæt ana        ealra monna
geþohtest þrymlice,        þristhycgende,
þæt þu þinne mægðhad        meotude brohtes,      15
sealdes butan synnum.        Nan swylc ne cwom
ænig oþer        ofer ealle men,
bryd beaghroden,        þe þa beorhtan lac
to heofonhame        hlutre mode
siþþan sende.        Forðon heht sigores fruma      20
his heahbodan        hider gefleogan
of his mægenþrymme        ond þe meahta sped
snude cyðan,        þæt þu sunu dryhtnes
þurh clæne gebyrd        cennan sceolde
monnum to miltse,        ond þe, maria, forð      25
efne unwemme        a gehealdan.
Eac we þæt gefrugnon        þæt gefyrn bi þe
soðfæst sægde        sum woðbora
in ealddagum,        esaias,
þæt he wære gelæded        þæt he lifes gesteald      30
in þam ecan ham        eal sceawode.
Wlat þa swa wisfæst        witga geond þeodland
oþþæt he gestarode        þær gestaþelad wæs
æþelic ingong.        Eal wæs gebunden

Thus the man of wisdom then looked around
until he saw where was established
a noble entrance. A huge door
was all decorated with precious treasure,
wound round with wondrous chains. He thought certainly
that none of human kind could ever
such firmly fixed bolts
to all eternity lift up,
or unlock the fastening of that city gate
until the angel of God with willing spirit
explained the matter and spoke these words:
"I may tell you," (that become true)
"that these golden gates yet at some time
God Himself, the Father Almighty, will
by the might of his spirit pass through,
and through these strong locks visit the earth,
and they after him will stand
eternally closed thus forever,
so that no other except God the Savior
may unlock them again."
Now is fulfilled that which the prophet then
looked on there with his eyes.
You are the gate, unique, through which the Ruling Lord
into this earth journied forth
and even thus Christ Almighty found you,
adorned with power, pure and set apart.
So after him the Lord of Angels,
the Giver of Life, locked you with a mysterious key
again undefiled by any thing.
Show us now the grace which to you the angel,
God's messenger Gabriel brought.
That indeed we mortals pray,
that you reveal to men that comfort,
your own Son. Afterward we may all
single-mindedly hope,

deoran since     duru ormæte,                  35
wundurclommum bewriþen.     Wende swiðe
þæt ænig elda     æfre *ne* meahte
swa fæstlice     forescyttelsas
on ecnesse     o inhebba*n*,
oþþe ðæs ceasterhlides     clustor onlucan,       40
ær him godes engel     þurh glædne geþonc
þa wisan onwrah     ond þæt word acwæð:
"Ic þe mæg secgan,"     (þæt soð gewearð)
"þæt ðas gyldnan gatu     giet sume siþe
god sylf wile     gæstes mægne               45
gefælsian,     fæder ælmihtig,
ond þurh þa fæstan locu     foldan neosan,
ond hio þonne æfter him     ece stond*að*
simle singales     swa beclysed
þæt nænig oþer,     nymðe nergend god,         50
hy æfre ma     eft onluceð."
Nu þæt is gefylled     þæt se froda þa
mid eagum þær     on wlatade.
Þu eart þæt wealldor,     þurh þe waldend frea
æne on þas eorðan     ut siðade,              55
ond efne swa þec gemette,     meahtum gehrodene,
clæne ond gecorene,     crist ælmihtig.
Swa ðe æfter him     engla þeoden
eft unmæle     ælces þinges
lioþucægan bileac,     lifes brytta.            60
Iowa us nu þa are     þe se engel þe,
godes spelboda,     gabriel brohte.
Huru þæs biddað     burgsittende
þæt ðu þa frofre     folcum cyðe,
þinre sylfre sunu.     Siþþan we mota*n*       65
anmodlice     ealle hyhtan,

now we look on that child at your breast.
Intercede for us now with vigorous words
that He not leave us any longer
in this valley of death to follow error,
but that He transport us into his Father's kingdom
where we sorrowless may ever
dwell in beatitude with the God of Hosts.

nu we on þæt bearn   foran breostum stariað.
Geþinga us nu   þristum wordum
þæt he us ne læte   leng owihte
in þisse deaðdene   gedwolan hyran,   70
ac þæt he usic geferge   in fæder rice,
þær we sorglease   siþþan motan
wunigan in wuldre   mid weoroda god.

3 *þe*, MS *e*, with preceding letter erased, but no new letter supplied.
11 *worlcundra*   18 *beaga hroden*   26 *gehealden*   32 *wisfœft*
37 *ne* not in MS   39 *inhebba*   48 *stondeð*   65 *motam*
73 *wunian*, with *g* squeezed in later below the line.

## X

O holy Lord of Heaven
you of old were with your Father
coexisting in that excellent home.
Not any angel was yet created,
nor any of that great mighty host
which up in the heavens watches over the kingdom,
God's magnificent dwelling and His service,
when you first were with the eternal Lord
yourself establishing this wide creation,
the broad earth-space. Common to you both is
the protecting Holy Spirit. We all, Savior Christ,
in humility pray you
that you hear the voice of captives,
of your servants, God the Savior,
how we are afflicted through our own willing.
Exiled wretches, evil spirits,
hateful hell-fiends have narrowly pressed us,
bound with dire ropes. The relief belongs
completely to you alone, eternal Lord.
Help the care-burdened, so that your advent
may comfort the miserable, although we against you
through our appetite for sin have carried on a feud.
Have mercy now on your servants and consider our misery,
how we totter with sickly spirits,
we wander abjectly. Come now, King of men,
do not delay too long. For us there is a need of grace,
that you save us and to us your salvation,
True One, give in order that we afterward
may always perform among men
the better thing, your will.

## X

Eala þu halga    heofona dryhten,
þu mid fæder þinne    gefyrn wære
efenwesende    in þam æþelan ham.
Næs ænig þa giet    engel geworden,
ne þæs miclan    mægenþrymmes nan           5
ðe in roderum up    rice biwitigað,
þeodnes þryðgesteald    ond his þegnunga,
þa þu ærest wære    mid þone ecan frean
sylf settende    þas sidan gesceaft,
brade brytengrundas.    Bæm inc is gemæne   10
heahgæst hleofæst.    We þe, hælend crist,
þurh eaðmedu    ealle biddað
þæt þu gehyre    hæfta stefne,
þinra *nie*dþiowa,    nergende god,
hu we sind geswencte    þurh ure sylfra gewill.   15
Habbað wræcmæcgas,    wergan gæstas,
hetl*a*n helsceaþ*a*n,    hearde genyrwa*d*,
gebunden bealorapum.    Is seo bot gelong
eall æt þe anum,    ece dryhten.
Hreowcearigum help,    þæt þin hidercyme   20
afrefre feasceafte,    þeah we fæhþo wið þec
þurh firena lust    gefremed hæbben.
Ara nu onbehtum    ond usse yrmþa geþenc,
Hu *w*e tealtrigað    tydran mode,
hwearfiað heanlice.    Cym nu, hæleþa cyning,   25
ne lata to lange.    Us is lissa þearf,
þæt þu us ahredde    ond us hælogiefe
soðfæst sylle,    þæt we siþþan forð
þa sellan þing    symle moten
geþeon on þeode,    þinne willan.   30

14 *medþiowa*    17 *hetlen helsceaþa*    17 *genyrwað*    24 *hu þe*

# XI

O beautiful, full of honor,
high and holy, heavenly Trinity,
widely worshipped throughout earthly plains,
whom rightfully the possessors of speech,
poor earth-bound men with all their might
should praise highly now that the faithful Savior
has revealed God to us that we may know Him.
Indeed they, the eager ones confirmed in glory,
the righteous race of seraphim
ever celebrating above among angels,
sing with unwearied strength,
exaltedly with loud voices,
beautifully far and near. They have the best
service with the King. Christ granted them
that they might with the eye enjoy his presence
forever without end, clothed with the sky,
might honor the Ruler far and wide
and with their wings shield the face
of the Almighty Lord, the eternal God,
and around the throne crowd eagerly,
whichever of them nearest our Savior
flying may flutter in that court of peace.
They praise the Precious One and to Him in light
these words speak, they glorify
the noble Originator of all creation:
"Holy art thou, holy, Prince of Archangels,
true Lord of Victory, ever art thou holy,
God of Gods. Always thy praise endures
on earth among men in every epoch
widely honored. Thou art the God of Hosts
since thou hast filled heaven and earth
with thy great glory, Protector of warriors,
Shield of all beings. To thee be in the highest
eternal glory and on earth praise,
bright among men. Live thou blessed
who in the name of the Lord came to men,
a solace to the lowly. To thee on high
be everlasting praise world without end."

# XI

Eala seo wlitige, weorðmynda full,
heah ond halig heofoncund þrynes,
brade geblissad geond brytenwongas
þa mid ryhte sculon reordberende,
earme eorðware, ealle mægene 5
hergan healice, nu us hælend god
wærfæst onwrah þæt we hine witan moton.
Forþon hy, dædhwæte, dome geswiðde,
þæt soðfæste seraphinnes cynn,
uppe mid englum a bremende, 10
unaþreotendum þrymmum singað
ful healice hludan stefne,
fægre feor ond neah. Habbaþ folgoþa
cyst mid cyninge. Him þæt crist forgeaf
þæt hy motan his ætwiste eagum brucan 15
simle singales, swegle gehyrste,
weorðian waldend wide ond side,
ond mid hyra fiþrum frean ælmihtges
onsyne weardiað, ecan dryhtnes,
ond ymb þeodenstol þringað georne 20
hwylc hyra nehst mæge ussum nergende
flihte lacan friðgeardum in.
Lofiað leoflicne ond in leohte him
þa word cweþað ond wuldriað
æþelne ordfruman ealra gesceafta: 25
"Halig eart þu, halig, heahengla brego,
soð sigores frea, simle þu bist halig,
dryhtna dryhten! A þin dom wunað
eorðlic mid ældum in ælce tid
wide geweorþad. Þu eart weoroda god, 30
forþon þu gefyldest foldan ond rodoras,
wigendra hleo, wuldres þines,
helm alwihta. Sie þe in heannessum
ece hælo, ond in eorþan lof,
beorht mid beornum. Þu gebletsad leofa, 35
þe in dryhtnes noman dugeþum cwome
heanum to hroþre. Þe in heahþum sie
a butan ende ece herenis."

7 *motan* corrected to *moton*   19 *wearð*   26 *brogo* corrected to *brego*

## XII

O, what a marvelous change in the life of men
that mankind's mild Creator
received from a virgin undefiled flesh!
She knew the love of man not at all
nor through seed of man on earth
came the Ruler of Victory; that was a greater feat
than all earth-dwellers comprehend
in its mysterious significance, how He, Glory of the skies,
High God of heaven, brought help
to man's kind through his mother's womb.
And thus continually going forth, the Savior of people,
the Lord of Hosts, every day grants
his forgiveness as an aid to men.
Therefore we eagerly in deeds and words
faithfully may praise him. That is the high counsel
to each man who has understanding,
that he always most often, most deeply
and most earnestly praise God.
He grants him the reward of His love,
the holy Savior himself,
even in the land where he never was before,
in the joy of the land of the living,
where he thereafter lives blessed,
dwells eternally, world without end.

        Amen.

# XII

*O admirabile commercium, Creator generis humani animatum corpus sumens, de virgine nasci dignatus est, et procedens homo sine semine, largitus est nobis suam deitatem.*

Eala hwæt, þæt is wræclic wrixl     in wera life
þætte moncynnes     milde scyppend
onfeng æt fæmnan     flæsc unwemme,
ond sio weres friga     wiht ne cuþe,
ne þurh sæd ne cwom     sigores agend     5
monnes ofer moldan;     ac þæt wæs ma cræft
þonne hit eorðbuend     ealle cuþan
þurh geryne,     hu he, rodera þrim,
heofona heahfrea,     helpe gefremede
monna cynne     þurh his modor hrif.     10
Ond swa forðgongende     folca nergend
his forgifnesse     gumum to helpe
dæleð dogra gehwam,     dryhten weoroda.
Forþon we hine domhwate     dædum ond wordum
hergen holdlice.     Þæt is healic ræd     15
monna gehwylcum     þe gemynd hafað,
þæt he symle oftost     ond inlocast
ond geornlicost     god weorþige.
He him þære lisse     lean forgildeð,
se gehalgoda     hælend sylfa,     20
efne in þam eðle     þær he ær ne cwom,
in lifgendra     londes wynne,     22
þær he gesælig     siþþan eardað
ealne widan feorh     wunað butan ende.

         Amen.

4 *niht*

notes

# POEM I

(See Bibliography for full citation of titles given in short form in Notes.)

Since the MS is imperfect at the beginning and we have no way of knowing how much has been lost, the exact nature of this poem is naturally uncertain. Comparing it with the Latin antiphon, it would appear that only the address, corresponding to the words *O Rex gentium, et desideratus earum,* has been lost. Judging from the poet's practice elsewhere, however, his adaptation of these words might have run anywhere from three to fifteen lines, and might have introduced wholly new material.

2-3 The idea of the stone rejected by the workmen goes back to sources much earlier than the antiphons. As Cook pointed out, it appears as early as the Psalms (117:22), from which it was picked up by New Testament writers (Matthew 21:42) and applied to Christ. In I Peter 2:7, the psalm is quoted directly.

7 *eorðbyrg.* The *g* is barely visible. The emendation *byrg,* or its less likely equivalent *byrig,* has been accepted by Holthausen, Grein, Cook, and others. The meaning of this entire line and the following one has remained relatively obscure to all editors, because *eall* is not the form we should expect if it is the subject of *wundrien,* and *gesihþe* gives rather awkward sense regardless of whether it be considered a dative singular or an accusative plural. Holthausen conjectures (*Literaturblatt* 21, 369-373) that a line is missing after line 8, and it would indeed be pleasant to think so. Gollancz translates the passage as plausibly as possible in the following way: "so that, throughout earth's cities, all things endowed with sight may wonder evermore, O Prince of Glory." *Wuldres Ealdor* is more idiomatic as a vocative than, as Cook suggests, an accusative with *wundrien.*

7b *ēagna.* An *n* is imperfectly erased in the MS after the final *a.*

8 *wundrien.* Kennedy (*Early English Christian Poetry,* p. 77) points out that this idea, not drawn from the antiphon, probably comes from either Psalm 117:23, Matthew 21:42, or Mark 12:10-11, which passages also use the cornerstone image.

10 *forlǣt.* Cook was unnecessarily bothered by this word. It fre-

quently carries the meaning of "leave standing" or "let remain."

11 *weall wið weall.* The two walls, connected in much Biblical commentary with the words *facit utraque unum* which appear in the antiphon (which took them from Ephesians 2: 14), were interpreted in Gregory's *Moralia* (Migne, *P.L.* 76, 459) as the Jews and the Gentiles, and again in the *Sensus Moralia* (Migne, *P.L.* 76, 467) as the active and the contemplative life. Cook gives quotations in full from Gregory and from Aelfric.

12 *cræftga.* The Exeter scribe, though an excellent one, was not above simple oversights now and then. By neglecting to put the cross stroke on the *f* (ꝼ), he left the letter an insular *s* (ſ).

15 *læmena.* If this word is an accusative plural to agree with *leomo*, it should have a *u* adjectival ending, and it was so emended by Grein. The MS reading should stand, however, because this sort of irregularity is natural and common in texts written in the tenth century. It could represent LWS confusion between back vowels in unstressed positions, or it could be an error introduced because of a mistaken connection with the *-ena* genitive plural ending.

15 *Līffrēa.* Sievers (PBB 10, 479) postulates an Anglian form *\*frega* for the second element of this compound, presumably to make this hemistich a normal member of the C type in his metrical system. It is of course possible that lines of this type do trace their origin to such disyllabic forms, but the monosyllabic *Frēa*, in this metrical situation, is so frequent that it is clear that it was accepted and used freely by poets long after it had ceased to be disyllabic. Perhaps this phenomenon, like so many other archaic elements of vocabulary, formulae, etc., was embraced as part of the body of conventionalized poetic tradition.

## POEM II

The ninth century liturgical writer Amalarius gives a commentary on the *O clavis* antiphon which perhaps explains the peculiar direction this Old English poem takes: "Haec antiphona aptatur gradui spiritus intellectus. Spiritus intellectus qui in Christo est, acumine luminis sui abdita penetrat et

NOTES

tenebras cordis inlustrat. Hoc enim agit qui, quando vult, aperit quod nemo potest claudere. Christus est lux vera, quae inluminat omnem hominem." *Liber de Ordine Antiphonarii* (*Studi e Testi 140*, Citta del Vaticano, 1950) p. 47.

1-4 These lines, apparently addressed to Christ, seem to reflect dimly something of the antiphon *O clavis David*. More obviously connected with this antiphon, however, are lines 47-51 of Poem IX. At line 5 the poet shifts his address to his audience.

2 *sē þe locan healdaþ*. Stanley B. Greenfield suggests very plausibly (MLN 67, 238-240) that this half line means "he who governs the locks," that is, the key. Kennings of this sort do not occur anywhere else in the Advent Lyrics, yet I incline to accept his interpretation. Previous editors and translators have taken the phrase to mean "he who holds the keys," but it is extremely unlikely that an Old English poet would show such manifest confusion as to use the word *loca* when he meant "key."

3 *ēadgan ūpwegas*. The word *ēadga* stands at the end of a MS line, immediately before a small triangular hole cut in the parchment. There is no way of being sure that an *n* was on the piece cut away, but there is no difficulty in understanding the text if it was, whereas *ēadga* presents grammatical problems. *ūpwegas* was first read by N. R. Ker from the ultraviolet photographs. See *Medium Aevum* 2, 225. Previous editors had read *ūs siges*, which yielded only several varieties of nonsense.

6-7 There have been no completely satisfactory reconstructions of the illegible text of these two lines. Grein conjectured *modgeomre halsigiað*; Gollancz, *nu gemærsigiað*; K-D (in a note) *monegiað*. The initial *m* of the word was not seen until ultraviolet photography revealed it. The K-D reading would seem to be the best, but the sense of this line depends materially on that of the next, which is much more hopeless. Grein suggested *hete heose sprecan*, but later revised this to *hete heofe sprecan*. Schipper (*Germania* 29, 329) suggested *hete to hofe sprecan*. Cook wisely refuses to speculate in such a case. The Facsimile edition reveals the last word to be *weorðan* rather than *sprecan*, thus rendering previous reconstructions vain. K-D, who also used the ultraviolet prints for this folio, think that *hete* looks more like *bete*. Kuhn (JEGP

{ 83 }

## NOTES

50, 491-493) reconstructs the lines: *þæt hē ne betēo tō tēose weorðan*. He argues very convincingly for his reading of the letters, but the sense he makes of the passage is strained and unlikely. Schaar (p. 72) rejects earlier readings and reconstructs thus: *þæt hē ne læte tō forlore weorðan*, which he translates: "that he may not suffer the crowd of the wretched to come to perdition." This makes good sense in the context, but the *forlore* is, as Schaar realizes, a sheer guess and rather too long for the space in the MS. The various problems remain unsolved, and I have preferred to leave the text without emendation.

9 *wēnað*. Editors before K-D had read *sunnan wilsīð*, but this reading gave doubtful sense. Cosijn (*Beiträge* 23, 109) was so disturbed that he imagined a lacuna after *sorgende*.

13 *gedō*. Cook and most of the editors and translators have taken this as an imperative, beginning an independent clause. The situation is awkward, however, for the preceding three lines have contained a series of optative verbs depending on *Līffrēa*, third person. Is it not unlikely that the poet would shift to an imperative verb, which addresses God directly in the second person, then in the second half line shift back to the third person (*hē*)? *Gedō* in this passage must rather be taken as another optative, parallel with *ontȳne, weorðe*, and *bewinde*, making the whole passage a sustained and effective bit of rhetorical parallelism.

14 *þā þe*. So reads the MS, although all editors since Thorpe have emended to *þā wē*. The *þ* and the *p* were often confused, to be sure, but the words can be a relative unit introducing a noun clause, object of *forlēt* (cf. v 12). I would translate: "May he make us worthy that He admitted to glory those who had to turn to this narrow land, bereft of home." The sense, of course, remains virtually the same, for in either case the poet is referring to the *ūs* group. *þĕ* in line 13 takes on a slightly different construction, but it is frequently found used in this way.

23 *gearnung*. Grein, dissatisfied with this word, suggested *geēacnung*, which Cook accepted into his text. There are two possible explanations of the form in the text as it stands, either of which makes emendation unnecessary. It could be a simple and understandable miswriting of *geearnung*, or it could be a rare, but not anomalous, form of *earnung*. *gea-* is sometimes

NOTES

written for *ēa* in several Mercian texts (Gregory's *Dialogues* O, Bede's *History* T, and the Blickling *Homilies*). See R. Vleeskruyer, *The Life of St. Chad*, Amsterdam, 1953, p. 57.

25 *geondsprēot*. See Introduction, p. 39.

## POEM III

The name Jerusalem was explained throughout the Middle Ages as meaning *pacis visio*. Modern Hebrew scholars agree that *salem* means "peace," but are not so sure of the meaning of the first element; they do not deny, however, that the medieval writers may have been right. Jerusalem had, of course, multiple meanings in the Biblical commentaries of the period, and some diversity of significance can be seen in the poem. Rhabanus Maurus in the ninth century explained the term thus: "Igitur praedictae quatuor figurae in unum ita si volumus confluunt, ut una eademque Hierusalem quadrifariam possit intelligi, secundum historiam civitas Judaeorum: secundum allegoriam Ecclesia Christi: secundum anagogen civitas Dei, illa coelestis, quae est mater omnium nostrum: secundum tropologiam anima hominis." (Migne, *P.L.* 112, 331.) Cook, in his article in the Festgabe for E. S. Sievers (*Philologische Studien*, Halle, 1890, p. 24), showed that a further meaning for Jerusalem was the Virgin Mary. Overtones of this significance are probably felt in lines 10-17 of this poem.

3 *þā āne*. Holthausen (*Literaturblatt* 21, 372) would emend here to *þāra þe āne*, but I think the MS reading can stand. *þā* can be considered an anticipatory article, or perhaps a pronoun (npf.), referring to *saule* in the next line. The meaning would then be: "And they alone (the souls of the just) in thee ever rest."

7 *firena*. All previous editors have read *firina*, and several have suggested emendation, but Ker (*Medium Aevum* 2, 226) reads this word in the ultraviolet print as *firena*.

8 *tō wuldre*. Klaeber (JEGP 4, 108) quotes several good parallels to show that this is an adverbial phrase meaning "gloriously."

9 *swā þū gehāten eart*. This seems to add another interpretation to the name Jerusalem (cf. note above). I can find no support in contemporary or earlier commentary for the connection of *halga hyht* with Jerusalem, except that, by definition, the heavenly Jerusalem is full of joy and hope.

{ 85 }

## NOTES

10-11 Although the drift is clear enough, this passage changes the meaning of *leva in circuitu oculos tuos* and presents several problems. Cook divided line 10 after *geond*, taking *þē geond* to equal *geond þē*. He goes on, however, to say that "the real difficulty is in the verb *geondwlītan*, for which one would like to substitute *geondwlīt*, parallel with *sioh*." Schaar (p. 73) accepts Holthausen's division after *þē* (*Literaturblatt* 21, 371), making *sylfa þē* equal *þē sylfa*. *geondwlītan* he would emend to *geondwlīte*, explaining that the scribe put on the *-an* because his eye caught the ending of *sīdan* in the line above. K-D say they understand the passage, but unfortunately they do not explain it to us. It seems clear to me that the passage must be emended in some manner to make normal and idiomatic Old English. I accept Schaar's *geondwlīte*, but since *sylfa þē* is excessively awkward, I would construe *þĕ* as a conjunction rather than as the personal pronoun. Thus I translate: "Look now yourself, that you may survey widely through the broad creation on every side and the roof of heaven, how. . . ."

15 *wordum*. The *d* was originally written *ð*, but later altered, probably by the same scribe. This sort of thing happens frequently in the Exeter Book.

18 *weorcum*. This word has sometimes mistakenly been interpreted as "work, labor," but the context clearly shows it to be the distinct word *weorc* (*wærc*), "pain, affliction."

20 *nīþum genēdde*. Here we may read *nīþum*, "enmities, malice," or it may be *nĭþum*, "men." Similarly, there are two possibilities for MS *geneðde*: the preterite of *geneðan*, "to venture," or past participle of *genēdan*, with one of the mistakenly crossed *d*'s which are so common in this text. See note 15 above. Scholars have made various combinations of these four possibilities. Gollancz translated: "he hath adventured him for men"; Kennedy and Cook seem to agree with him, although rather hesitantly. Klaeber (JEGP 4, 108) argued convincingly for "forced by hostility," and Bright, Schaar, and K-D appear to agree. In this case, *genēdde* must modify *benda* and we must stretch its usual meaning to something like Bright's "imposed by sin (iniquities)."

# POEM IV

There is an interlinear gloss in the MS for the first seven lines of this poem. Chambers (Facsimile, p. 91) identified the hand as that of Lawrence Nowell, dean of Lichfield (d. 1576). Between this poem and the preceding, he wrote in the space skipped by the OE scribe: *Hymnus in laudē virginis Mariæ*. His glossing goes word for word as follows: "O womans frend thrugh glories maistie (*power* written above) virgine most/ free (*ofer ealne foldan sceat* left untranslated) that ever earthly/ inhabitantes say heard declare to us the mysterie which to the/ frō heaven how thou conception receavedest of a child/ thurgh the birth———the compagnie after mans maner of minde/ diddest not knowe Nor we truely suche thīges never knewe in times passed/ ever to channce w$^{che}$ thou in singuler gift or grace suche diddest receave."

1 *wuldres þrym*. This phrase cannot have the same meaning it does at line 13 below. Cook believed it meant "heavenly glory, heaven," and he assumed that the poem was addressed to Mary in heaven. Kennedy translates: "in the host of heaven." I take the phrase here to be simply a superlative exaltation of Mary: "beyond all glory noblest woman" or "exceeding the glory of glories." Kennedy's translation of *þrym* is possible, however, and the phrase might mean "among the multitude of the glorious."

3 *þæs þe*. Cook's note indicates that this connective must be translated "as far as." I suspect it means simply "of whom," as Gordon and Gollancz translate it.

3 *sundbūend*. This compound is formed on the pattern of *eorðbūend*, *foldbūend*, etc. and has similar meaning. The first element is obviously *sund*, sea (see Cosijn Beiträge 23, 109-130), but as it is used here and in the Meters of Boethius, it seems to mean "men" in general, rather than specifically maritime dwellers.

5 I feel sure that the poet must be using *ēacnung* and *onfōn* with deliberately dual meanings, for both words have rather specialized meanings concerned with conception as well as the more usual generalized significance indicated in the translation.

6 *bearnes þurh gebyrde*. This poetic idiom was a favorite of our poet. It is the equivalent of *þurh bearnes gebyrde*.

## NOTES

7 *mōd*. This word has caused much perplexity, probably because of a misconstruction placed upon the preceding word. Thorpe in a note queries *mode?* and translates "in mind." Grein would emend to *mōt*, meeting. Cook puts forward an elaborate argument for *mot*, atom, mote, thereby creating an OE idiom, almost out of whole cloth. K-D correctly point out that *mōd* can be the accusative object of *æfter*, but do not go on to explain that the trouble has lain with *monwīsan*. The word occurs elsewhere only in the Old English *Genesis* 1939, but it obviously cannot have the same usage or meaning here that it does there, however we interpret the passage. Most editors have tried to take it as a noun, but it is far more likely that it is a word formed with the common *-wīs* adjectival suffix, and that it means "human, manlike." The whole phrase would then mean "according to man's mind," or "according to human ideas"; thus Gollancz' "after human fashion" and Lawrence Nowell's "after mans maner of minde" were not far from right.

14-15 The idea of the eternal virginity is not found in the *O virgo virginum*, but it occurs in another nativity antiphon: "Virgo mansit et post partum. . . . Hodie processit proli magnifici germinis, et perseverat pudor virginitatis, alleluia."

16 Cook considered this passage puzzling and impertinent, but it is of a piece with the earlier part of this speech. See Introduction, p. 18.

21 *sunu*. The antiphon mentions only *filiae Jerusalem*.

21 *Sōlimae*. The Latin *Solyma* was a shortened form of *Hierosolyma*. The poet here even used the Latin genitive case ending.

23 *mund*. No one has found a thoroughly satisfactory explanation for this word, although it is distinctly in a defining context. Dietrich suggested (*Haupts Zeitschrift* 7, 184) that it was a borrowing from the Old Norse meaning "moderation, chastity." His evidence is strained and doubtful, but Cook and Grein accepted his explanation. My guess is that it is a nonce borrowing (similar to *culpan* VII 14) of the Latin *mundus*, which when used substantively in ecclesiastical works means "cleanliness, freedom from sin."

24 *mǣre*. This adjective clearly modifies *mōdor*. Cook emended to *mǣran* in order to make it modify *suna*.

28 *wærgða*. Originally written *wærða*, then later a *g* was squeezed

## NOTES

in below the line, apparently by the same hand. This sort of thing happened often in the early part of the Exeter Book.

## POEM V

1 *Éarendel*. This word has been controversial, principally because it is rare. It glosses the Latin *jubar* in the Epinal and Erfurt glossaries, and would thus seem to mean "splendor, brilliance." It would therefore be a better translation for *splendor lucis aeternae* than *Oriens*. However, it is also used as the *glossa* for *Aurora* in two glossed OE hymns (*Surtees Hymns* 16, 18; 30, 1). In both meanings, it is obviously connected with light, and since in these instances light is used figuratively for God's light, perhaps Cook's debate between "dawn," "day star," or "sun" is too literal to be to the point. He, and most of the poem's translators, find it difficult to separate the word from the Latin *Oriens*, which they understand better than the OE word. Part of the interest in the word is in its etymological connection with early Germanic legend, for it seems to be a cognate for the Norse *Ørvandil*, about whom there is an interesting astronomical legend. (See Finnur Jónsson, *Edda Snorra Sturlusonar*, Reykjavik, 1903, p. 141.) Since the word, judging from its rarity, was dying out in Old English, it is likely that consciousness of its legendary connections had died earlier.

6 *god of gode*. Cook noticed that these words (and he might have added the whole passage to line 24) have affinities with the Nicene Creed, which is said at every Mass: "Credo . . . in unum dominum Jesum Christum, Filium Dei unigenitum, et ex Patre natum ante omnia saecula, *Deum de Deo*, Lumen de Lumine, Deum vero de Deo vero, genitum non factum, consubstantialem Patri, per quem omnia facta sunt. Qui propter nos homines et propter nostram salutem descendit de coelis, et incarnatus est de Spiritu Sancto ex Maria virgine, et homo factus est." Besides the creed, however, Burgert (p. 87) points out that an antiphon sometimes used on Christmas day reads as follows: "Natus est nobis deus de deo, lumen de lumine, quod erat in principio."

6 *gēaro*. This is almost certainly the same as *gēara*, of old, although Cook and others, in spite of the lame sense, have taken it as *gearo*.

## NOTES

10 *þurh byldo*. This whole phrase acts as an adverbial unit meaning "confidently, boldly." Some translators, following Grein, have rendered it "with constancy."

11 *þē sylf*. Thorpe in a note suggested that this should be *þū sylf*.

17 *brungen*. The passage is clear if we take this as modifying *hǣlo*.

18 *ælmihtigum*. Holthausen (*Anglia Beiblatt* 9, 356) states that the meter craves the form *ælmihtgum*. I retain the MS reading, mainly because the spellings *-ig-* and *-g-* are insignificant orthographic variants, and even if an OE reader spoke this half line as a perfect Sievers type A, he might have written it as we find it here.

25 *bi gewyrhtum*. Klaeber (JEGP 4, 109) disliked the translation "by our deeds" and suggested that a better one is *merito*, "as we ought." Gollancz was following this idea when he translated it "as it is meet."

## POEM VI

Cook points out that an antiphon very similar to the *O Emmanuel* is sung at Lauds on Thursday of the third week of Advent: "Dominus legifer noster, Dominus rex noster; ipse veniet et salvabit nos." Both antiphons are drawn from Isaiah 33:22. I do not find reference to this second antiphon in the early authorities, however, and it may have come into use after the date of our poem.

4 *ǣrest*. Isaiah, rather than Gabriel, was of course the first to call Christ Emmanuel. This error Burgert (p. 87) claimed to have been carried over from the antiphonary in use in the poet's monastery. The text of the *O Gabriel* antiphon (see p. 8) could also have been his source for this confusion.

8-9 *sācerd . . . Melchisedech*. These lines are clearer if we remember that Melchisedech (Genesis 14:18) was a *rex Salem* and *sacerdos Dei altissimi*. He was later taken as the archetype of perfect priests (Psalms 109:4) and still later by the author of the Epistle to the Hebrews as a forerunner of Christ. In so far as he was a manifestation of the spirit of Christ, it would be said that he *godþrym onwrāh*, as did Christ. "Melchisedech . . . rex Salem, quod est, rex pacis, sine patre, sine matre, sine genealogia, neque initium dierum, neque finem vitae habens, assimilatus autem Filio Dei, manent sacerdos in perpetuum." (Hebrews 7:1-3) The *Glossa*

### NOTES

*Ordinaria*, which collects most of the earlier doctrine of the Fathers, comments on this passage: "Melchisedech, qui interpretatur rex justitiae et rex pacis, Christum significat, per quem reconciliati sumus, et qui in fine saeculi juste judicaturus est." (Migne, *P.L.* 113, col. 120).

18 The poet here has introduced the Harrowing of Hell motif, which very well might have been drawn from the hint in the *O Rex pacifice* antiphon.

24 Sievers (*Beiträge* 10, 453) conjectured *for* to fill the illegible gap. Holthausen, followed by Cook, proposed *æfter*. Schaar (p. 74) suggests *hēr for oferþearfum*, which would be about right from the point of view of the space in the MS.

25 Grein emended this damaged spot to *gesōhtest*; Gollancz, followed by Cook, conjectured *gesece*. The Facsimile edition reported that *es ne læt* was visible in the ultraviolet print, which reading is very near to Thorpe's (*es nu læt*) of over a hundred years ago. K-D and Schaar accept the emendation *geseces*, but since this produces an awkward shift of mood in the verbs, I prefer to leave the matter unsettled, as it most certainly is.

## POEM VII

This dialogue has no source in the antiphons, and it appears to be original with the poet. Cook (JEGP 4, 421-451) unearthed several analogues for this sort of dramatic dialogue between Joseph and Mary, four in Greek homilies and one in the Latin Pseudo-Augustine. These are mainly works of doubtful authorship and uncertain date, but three of them are probably earlier than the date of our poem. Several show some attempt to penetrate the psychology of Joseph, perhaps the most interesting being the Pseudo-Augustine, which our poet presumably could have read if it came into his way. Cook in his edition also notes the similarities to the thirteenth and fourteenth chapters of the Apocryphal Gospel of St. James (*The Apocryphal New Testament*, ed. M. R. James, Oxford, 1953), a fact later "discovered" by M. M. Dubois (*Les Elements Latins dans la Poesie Religieuse de Cynewulf*, Paris, 1943). None of these parallels can be considered sources, however, and they merely show that other writers had similar imaginative perceptions of the scene in which

Joseph confronts Mary; all of them were stimulated by a single germinal verse in the Gospel of St. Matthew (1:19). Until a closer source is found, we are allowed to believe our poet invented this dialogue for purposes of instruction. See Introduction, p. 22.

1. Lawrence Nowell supplied an interlinear gloss in the MS for the first four lines of this poem as follows: "O Joseph mine Jocobes child kinsman of David/ the great king now thou [*freode* untranslated] shalt [*fæste gedæ/ lan alætan lufan mine* untranslated] I long am greatly vex:/ ed of iugement bereft."

1 *Iacobes bearn.* Joseph's actual father was named Jacob (Matthew 1:16) but this may be a reference to Joseph's being of the lineage of the earlier patriarch, Jacob.

6 *worda.* K-D suggest that the MS *worde* may be retained as an instrumental, "in word," but I follow Thorpe, Grein, and Cook in emending to the genitive plural. *Worn* normally takes a genitive, and this word certainly looks like a natural parallel for *sorga* and *sārcwida*. We would have an anomalous mixed construction if *worn* governed both an instrumental and two genitives. See p. 42.

12 *Ēalā fæmne geong.* Cosijn (*Beiträge* 23, 109) felt this sort of ending to a speech improbable, and suggested a different speech arrangement. He would have had Mary's first speech run to line 12 (changing *for þē* in 1. 6 to *for þȳ* and *fēasceaftne* in 1. 12 to *fēasceafte*), Joseph's speech from 1. 12b to 1. 32a, and Mary's final speech from there to the end. Cook (pp. 97-98) argues cogently against this arrangement. S. B. Hemingway (MLN 22, 62-63) suggested a different arrangement: he would begin a new speech at 1. 10, putting the sentence *God ēaþe mæg . . . fēasceafte* (besides emending this word, he would change *mīnre* in 1. 11 to *þīnre*) into the mouth of Mary. The *Ēalā fæmne geong* would then be Joseph's "exclamation of despair." I have retained the traditional arrangement, since it forms a cogent and understandable exchange without emendations, with far more imaginative emotional content than that provided by the emenders.

25 *womma lēase ond nū gehwyrfed is.* The alliteration in this line has troubled several editors. Rieger (*Alt-und-Angelsächsisches Lesebuch*, Giessen, 1861, p. 117) assumed the loss of

two half lines, and composed some original Old English to supply the imagined gap. Grein reads *gewyrped* instead of *gehwyrfed*, and Holthausen (*Literaturblatt* 21, 369-373) suggests *gewyrfed*. The alliteration indeed was probably on *w*, but the MS reading is quite acceptable if we remember that even after *h* was lost as a distinct sound in some of these *h* plus consonant words, the older spelling remained. (See Luick, § 704, a.1.)

26 *purh nāthwylces*. The MS gives no indication of it, but there is something definitely wrong with this half line, in that *purh* cannot take a genitive object. Körner (*Angelsächsische Texte*, 1880) emended the word to *nāthwylcne*; Grein suggested *nāthwylces searo*; Cosijn (*Beiträge* 23, 110) proposed *nāthwylces nīð*; Schaar (p. 24) favored *nāthwylces mān*. Gollancz plausibly suggested that the error may "be explained as a confusion of two constructions; *purh nat-hwylcne* (the accusative after *purh*), and *nát hwylces* (the gen. after *nát*; cf. *nāt hē pāra gōda*, Beow. 682)." Though Gollancz doesn't say so, this mistake, if it occurred, was probably not the poet's but rather some transcriber's. In any case, the solecism produced does not obscure the general idea of the line.

29b-30a Although I cannot agree with Bourauel that the passage from St. Jerome's *Commentariorum in Evangelium Matthaei* was a source of this dialogue, yet one remark of Jerome helps explain Joseph's dilemma: "Et in lege praeceptum est, non solum reos, sed et conscios criminum obnoxios esse peccati (Levit. V): quomodo Joseph cum crimen celit [Al. celaret] uxoris, justos scribitur." (Migne, *P.L.* 26, col. 25).

43-45 The punctuation of this passage I owe to Schaar (p. 74). The *nū-nū* construction in these lines is probably correlative and causal.

## POEM VIII

2 *ealra cyninga cyning*. Bourauel noted that an antiphon for Matins on the Vigil of Christmas reads: "Magnificatus est Rex pacificus super omnes reges universae terrae." (Migne, *P.L.* 78, 733.)

3-4 The idea of the eternal coexistence of the Father and the Son is one which is frequently emphasized in various forms in many of the ordinary antiphons of the Advent season. The words *Ego hodie genui te* appear in antiphons used at Christmas and at Epiphany. See *Liber Antiphonarius*, Migne, *P.L.* 78, 646, 649.

6-10 Bourauel points out that a response for the third nocturn at Vespers on the Vigil of Christmas reads: "Hic qui advenit nemo scit naturam ejus, nisi ipse solus." See Migne, *P.L.* 78, 735. This idea appears again in these poems at XII 7.

18 *geféa*. Holthausen (*Literaturblatt* 21, 371), Sedgefield (*Anglo-Saxon Verse Book*, Manchester, 1922, p. 99) and Bright (quoted by Cook) have favored deleting this word. It does create a metrical anomaly, and the sense is satisfactory without it. It *is* there in the MS, however, and the sense is also quite satisfactory with it there. Emendations for metrical reasons tacitly assume that we understand what metrical anomalies were not allowable better than the tenth century scribe who wrote our MSS.

22 *æfterþon*. Grein, Gollancz, and Cook print this as *æfter þon*, apparently not disturbed that *þon*, as an article, is in the instrumental case but modifies a noun in the accusative. K-D suggest that *æfterþon* is a compound word and perhaps should be considered analogous to *ǣrþon*. Unfortunately, the *ǣrþon* they use for analogy (l. 25 of this poem) is obviously a conjunction rather than a preposition. It does seem likely that this compound preposition did exist in Old English, however, although Sweet's *Student's Anglo-Saxon Dictionary* is the only dictionary which lists it.

26-27. This is a clear statement of the ancient and orthodox doctrine that Christ is the *sapientia* by which all things, including the original creation, are effected. Cook believed that these lines have some connection with another of the O antiphons, the O Sapientia. See Introduction, p. 6. Aside from the single word *snyttro*, I see no connection with this antiphon. Burgert (p. 51) indicated a belief that a poem based on the O Sapientia was among the material lost at the beginning of the series of poems.

38 *gyldnan geatu*. This metaphor for the physical birth from Mary's womb was a rhetorical commonplace in hymns and commentaries as well as the liturgy. A Latin hymn containing several ideas which recur in these Advent poems is printed in *Latin Hymns of the Anglo-Saxon Church*, ed. J. Stevenson, London, p. 112:

## NOTES

> Fit porta Christo pervia
> Referta plena gratia
> Transitque rex et permanet
> Clausa ut fuit persecula.

Cook quotes two responds from Gregory's *Liber Responsalis*:

"Introivit per aurem Virginis in regionem nostram, indutus stolam purpuream. Et exivit per auream portam lux et decus universae fabricae mundi," and "Ingressus est per splendidam regionem, aurem Virginis, visitare palatium uteri; et regressus est per auream Virginis portam." (Migne, *P.L.* 78, 734, 731.)

43 *wulf*. The devil is not referred to in any of the antiphons, and indeed does not figure largely in any part of the Advent office. There is one reference in one of the *Orationes de Adventu Domini quotidianis diebus* which are contained in Gregory's *Liber Sacramentorum* (Migne, *P.L.* 78, 196): "Festina, ne tardaveris, Domine Deus noster, et a diabolico furore nos potenter libera."

44 *dēor dǣdscuan*. Cook accepted Cosijn's suggestion and emended this to *deorc dēaðscua*, which may have been a formulaic phrase (cf. Beowulf 160 and similar phrases in Psalms 87:6; 106:9-13, Christ and Satan 453). I prefer to stay closer to the MS reading, following Grein, Gollancz, and Assmann, but if the whole phrase is going to mean "beast of darkest deed" (Gollancz) or "beast of shadowy deeds," it needs the *n* which I have supplied in order to make it a genitive.

48 *usse*. This is, as Cook indicates, the genitive form, more normally spelled *ussa*, but no emendation is necessary since late texts often show such reduced final vowels.

51 *wītes*. There is some doubt as to whether this should be read *wītes bona*, "slayer of torture" or "torturing slayer," or *wites* (*wittes*) *bona*, "slayer of the mind or spirit." Neither phrase occurs in other OE poems, although compounds with similar ideas, *gāstbona* and *sūslbona*, can be cited in support of either interpretation. I follow Cook and Sievers (*Beiträge* 10, 456) in interpreting the word as *wītes*. Whatever the precise meaning, it is clearly a kenning for the devil.

57 *fortylde*. I cannot accept Cosijn's emendation *fortyhte* (*Beiträge* 22, 110). As K-D indicate, this *hapax legomenon* derives from *\*tillan*, "to touch, reach," which appears in OE

{ 95 }

only in such compounds as *ātillan* and *getillan*. (See Bosworth-Toller.) The root is well attested, having cognates in Old Frisian and Dutch, and when combined with the *for-* intensive prefix, it would produce just the meaning this context seems to require.

## POEM IX

1 *mǣra*. K-D p. 48n. note that even if the weak adjective used as a substantive in the vocative case can be admitted here, we should still expect the feminine form *mǣre*. Probably the MS spelling, however, merely represents the weakened tenth century pronunciation in the guise of a hyperform. Thorpe thought this a scribal error for *Maria*.

18 *bēaghroden*. Holthausen (*Anglia Beiblatt* 9, 355) first proposed to change the MS *beaga hroden* to *bēaghroden* for metrical reasons. A better motive is that the compound is very frequently applied to women in OE poetry, whereas the verb with the genitive construction would be anomalous. Cook pointed out that *hrēodan*, when used with a dependent noun, takes the instrumental case rather than the genitive.

29 *Ēsaīas*. The poet is obviously referring to Ezekiel's vision of the temple, reported in the Book of Ezekiel 44:1-2. Cook points out that the service for Wednesday of the first week of Advent in the Roman Breviary has the following response after the second lesson: "Ante multum tempum prophetavit Ezechiel: Vidi portam clausam; ecce Deus ante saecula ex ea procedebat pro salute mundi; et erat iterum clausa, demonstrans virginem, quia post partum permansit virgo." This response obviously makes use of the same concepts and imagery which appear in two of our Advent antiphons, *O Rex pacifice* and *O clavis David*. In any case, the source is transmuted and the passage becomes typically Old English in its intricate elaboration. As to the mistake of Isaiah for Ezekiel, Cook suggests that the poet might have become confused, since the lesson immediately preceding this response comes from Isaiah. Indeed, Cook might have added that virtually all the daily lessons during Advent come from Isaiah. It also seems possible that the poet ascribed the vision to Isaiah simply because his book is more directly connected in most Christian minds with Mary and the Advent; the mistake would be

understandable in these terms if the poet were working not from written sources but from his own accumulation of ideas, impressions, and emotions. See Introduction, p. 35.

30b *þæt*. Thorpe, Cosijn, and Cook emended this word to *þǣr*, which certainly does improve a poorly written sentence. *þæt*, "so that," is idiomatic and meaningful, however, and I refuse to "improve" our author unless there is concrete evidence that the scribes have not transmitted what he wrote.

37 *elda*. Prompted by a normalizing tendency, Cook emends to *ælda*. *elda*, however, is not only the Kentish form but it frequently appears in poetry which is predominantly Anglian.

37 *ne*. Thorpe first suggested inserting this *ne* into the text. Grein, Assmann, Cook, and K-D have accepted the emendation, but recently Schaar (p. 75) has argued for retaining the MS reading *ǣfre meahte*, as did Gollancz, who translates: "he pondered deeply, how any mortal man might ever raise those bolts, etc." This interpretation is unsound, in my opinion, because it has to ring in a nonexistent "how" to keep the expression positive and also it translates *wēnan* as "ponder, consider" rather than "have an opinion, expect," which are its normal meanings. For Gollancz' sense, an Old English writer would probably have used the word *smēagan*.

39 *inhebban*. See p. 40n.

46 *gefælsian*. In an article (JEGP 1, 334-337), Cook put forth good evidence for the meaning "pass through" for this word. Thorpe, Grein, and Gollancz, using such senses as "make pure" and "make resplendent," had produced nothing but nonsense from the passage.

67 *foran*. Previous editors have put this word at the end of the first half line. All of them, however, seem to take it as a preposition with *brēostum* as its object; as such it seems extremely awkward in a stressed position in the first hemistich. If it be objected that the present division adds unwelcome anacrusis to a neat Sievers A line, I can only respond that, of two evils, this at least does not have metrics and syntax in open conflict.

68ff. It is clear that the poet, following the pattern of the other antiphons, has adapted the *veni ad salvandum nos* motif as a petition for intercession.

NOTES

## POEM X

9 This idea appears also at VIII 27, where it also reminds the audience that the Babe of Bethlehem was a cosmic force.

11 In this line we have the most concrete reference in all the series to the Holy Trinity.

17 *hetlan helsceaþan.* Gollancz, Grein, and K-D notwithstanding, the MS *hetlen helsceaþa* cannot stand without some sort of emendation. To be a parallel subject of *habbað*, *helsceaþa* certainly needs to be plural. It also seems unlikely that the adjective *hetlen* ever existed; the *-en*, to be sure, is an acceptable adjectival ending, but nowhere in Old English have I been able to discover that it is added directly to another adjective meaning the same thing. I agree with Thorpe, Cook, and Cosijn (*Beiträge* 22, 110) that we have here simply the common adjective *hetol*, declined weak. We can reduce Cook's changes slightly if we assume that the phonetically reduced middle syllable dropped out: *\*hetolan > hetlan.* See Luick, § 336. The final syllable shows the normal weakening toward [ə].

26 *ne lata tō lange.* These words and the phrase *þæt þū ūs ahrēdde* are the only passages Cook used as evidence for his suggestion that this poem is based on the antiphon *O radix Jesse.* A. A. May (MLN 24, 158-159) claimed that *O Sapientia* is a more likely source, since lines 1-7 reflect *Primogenita ante omnem creaturam* from Ecclesiastes 24: 5, the Biblical source for part of *O Sapientia.* Lines 8-9, he claims, reflect *fortiter suaviterque disponens omnia.* The words *ne lata tō lange* May claimed could have come from *Festina, ne tardaveris, Domine,* a versicle which immediately precedes *O Sapientia* in the service. Burgert disagreed with these claims, pointing out that the versicle in question, and its response, were sung, not just before the *O Sapientia,* but before each of the antiphons, and thus even if influential, were not to be used as an argument for *O Sapientia* as a source. Burgert proposed that the poet was in this poem writing "his own final 'O.' " Certain ideas in the poem he thought influenced by the Preface to the Midnight Mass on Christmas, plus a prayer from the office for a later Mass and another prayer from the observance of Ember Saturday in Advent. The ideas in these prayers were commonplaces, however, and the poet had probably

{ 98 }

learned them as a child with his catechism. See Introduction, p. 35.

## POEM XI

Cook thought this poem based on two antiphons to the Trinity, and Burgert emended his idea, but I am willing to drop it altogether. Burgert (p. 45) also thought the first 25 lines of the poem were influenced by an antiphon which is now used in the Votive Office of the Angels: "Laudemus Dominum, quem laudant angeli, quem cherubim et seraphim Sanctus, Sanctus, Sanctus proclamant." There is no question about lines 26-38, which are manifestly based on the *Sanctus* and *Benedictus* of the Mass. I would further suggest that the earlier part of the poem is based, in the free manner the poet often uses with his sources, on the preface which immediately precedes the *Sanctus*. Cook quotes part of it (p. 111), but unaccountably does not stress its importance. The full text in Gregory's *Liber Sacramentorum* runs:

> Vere dignum et justum est, aequum et salutare, nos tibi semper et ubique gratias agere, Domine sancte, Pater omnipotens, aeterne Deus, per Christum Dominum nostrum. Per quem Majestatem tuam laudant angeli, adorant dominationes, tremunt potestates: coeli, coelorumque virtutes, ac beata seraphim socia exsultatione concelebrant. Cum quibus et nostras voces, ut admitti jubeas, deprecamur, supplici confessione dicentes: Sanctus, Sanctus, Sanctus, Dominus Deus Sabaoth. Pleni sunt coeli et terra gloria tua, Osanna in excelsis. Benedictus qui venit in nomine Domini. Osanna in excelsis.
> (Migne, *P.L.* 78, 25)

Burgert claimed that the special preface for one of the Christmas Masses influenced the preceding poem; this, however, was the common preface, used at every Mass except when there was a festal service with a specially appointed preface. Bourauel (pp. 99-100) believed that l. 7 shows that the poet had before him the preface to the second Christmas Mass (Migne, *P.L.* 78, 31), which contains the words *clara nobis omnia et intellectu manifestavit, et visu*, but I question whether, even if he knew these words, he had any text "before him."

4 *þā*. Cook alone emends this word to *þec*; all other editors have kept the MS reading, taking *þā* as a relative pronoun and assuming an unexpressed object for *hergan*.

4 *mid rihte*. Cook believed that this translated the word *Jure* in one of the Trinity antiphons he claimed to be the source of this poem, but surely the *justum est* of the preface quoted above is as good a source.

9 *seraphinnes*. Here Cook introduced quotations from Aelfric (as he does anent the *þrȳnes* at line 2) which prove little except that the Anglo-Saxons were familiar with the accepted Christian doctrine. The picture of the angels here is conventional, albeit vividly recreated by the OE poet, and goes back ultimately to such passages in the Bible as Isaiah 6: 2. Comparable poetic adaptations are to be found in *Andreas* 719-724 and *Elene* 739-749.

19 *weardiað*. All editors, from Thorpe onward, have agreed that the poet must have originally written *weardiað* instead of the MS *wearð*.

37 *sīe*. Holthausen (*Anglia Beiblatt* 9, 355-358) states that the meter demands *sȳ* instead of *sīe*, but most metrists today would allow the diphthong in *sīe* to be monosyllabic.

## POEM XII

Samuel Moore in 1914 noted (MLN 29, 226) that the first six lines of this poem were based on the antiphon *O admirabile commercium*, which is sung at Lauds and Vespers on the feast of the Circumcision and at Lauds on the Vigil of the Epiphany. This antiphon, which thus belongs to the end of the Christmas season, appropriately brings this Advent series to a close. Burgert tried unsuccessfully to show that there is a connection with the antiphon up through line 13.

1 *Ēalā Hwæt*. These words combine the conventional OE *Hwæt* opening formula with the *Ēalā* formula which has been used for these hymns. This gives extra solemnity and emphasis to the beginning of this poem and is an effective warning of the approach to the end. Both words are extrametrical, unlike the *Ēalā*'s of the earlier poems, and are not to be considered in the Sieversian scansion of the line.

4 *wiht*. All editors correct this mistake. The scribe possibly misread the minims of *uiht* as *niht*.

## NOTES

6 *monnes*. This modifies *sæd* and is not parallel with *sigores*.

6 *mā*. Sievers suggested that this should read *māra* (*metri causa*) (PPB 10, 515) and Cook accepted the emendation. I follow all the other editors in accepting the MS reading, for metrical irregularities of this sort are by no means infrequent, and probably reflect the fact that by the period of this poem, poetry of this sort was visual as well as oral.

12 *forgifnesse*. I find no support for Cook's meaning of "bounty, largesse," although Burgert eagerly accepts it. In all the occurrences I have found, the word means "forgiveness" or something very near to it.

17 *inlocast*. This is probably a form of *inlicost*, where the medial vowel has assumed a reduced sound ([e]?) and has been given a nonce spelling of *o*. See Cook, p. 113.

22ff. Schaar (p. 296) finds the final lines very similar to the final lines of Guthlac A: "But it is impossible to say which passage is imitated from the other; one of them is no doubt a borrowing." I doubt it. The parallel hemistichs, as well as the general tone of termination of the two passages, are patently part of the OE stock of formulas and prove absolutely nothing about borrowing. Schaar's error is the more puzzling when he goes ahead in the next paragraph (p. 297) to another set of parallels between Christ and Beowulf and says: "They may be considered formulary turns of expression." His failure to draw a clear line between borrowing and "formulary" expression is also evident in a recent article ("On a New Theory Of Old English Poetic Diction," *Neophilologus* 4, 301-305).

# bibliography

# Bibliography

(Short titles used for frequent citations are given in parentheses after each item.)

### Complete Editions of the Advent Lyrics

Benjamin Thorpe, *Codex Exoniensis*, London, 1842. (THORPE)
C. W. M. Grein, *Bibliothek der angelsächsischen Poesie*, 4 v., Göttingen, 1857-1864. (GREIN)
Israel Gollancz, *Cynewulf's Christ*, London, 1892. (GOLLANCZ)
Israel Gollancz, *The Exeter Book*, Part I (EETS 104), London, 1895.
R. P. Wülker, ed., *Bibliothek der angelsächsischen Poesie*, Kassel, 1883-1898. (ASSMANN)
A. S. Cook, *The Christ of Cynewulf*, Boston, 1900 (COOK)
R. W. Chambers, et al., *The Exeter Book of Old English Poetry*, London, 1933. (FACSIMILE)
G. P. Krapp and E. V. K. Dobbie, *The Exeter Book*, New York, 1936. (K-D)

### Complete Translations

(Thorpe and Gollancz included translations in each of their editions cited above.)
C. H. Whitman, *The Christ of Cynewulf*, Boston, 1900. (WHITMAN)
C. W. Kennedy, *The Poems of Cynewulf*, London, 1910. (KENNEDY)
R. K. Gordon, *Anglo-Saxon Poetry*, London, 1927. (GORDON)

### Secondary Material

A. R. Benham, "Christ 117 and 125b-127a," JEGP 7 (1907), 110.
Gustav Binz, *Untersuchungen zum altenglischen sogenannten Crist*, Leipzig, 1907.
F. A. Blackburn, "Is the 'Christ' of Cynewulf a single poem?", *Anglia* 19 (1897), 89-98.
Johannes Bourauel, *Zur Quellen-und-Verfasserfrage von Andreas Crist und Fata*, Bonner Beiblatt zur Anglistik 11 (1901), 65-132.

## BIBLIOGRAPHY

A. Brandl (Review of Cook), *Archiv* 111 (1903), 447-449.

C. F. Brown, "Cynewulf and Alcuin," PMLA 18 (1903), 308-334.

Edward Burgert, *The Dependence of Part I of Cynewulf's Christ upon the Antiphonary*, Washington, 1921.

J. J. Campbell, "Structural Patterns in the Old English Advent Lyrics," ELH 23 (1956), 239-255.

R. W. Chambers, "The British Museum Transcript of the Exeter Book," *Anglia* 35 (1912), 393-400.

A. S. Cook, "A Remote Analogue to the Miracle Play," JEGP 4 (1903), 421-425.

A. S. Cook, "Christ 77," JEGP 1 (1897), 247-248.

A. S. Cook, "Notes on the Old English Christ," JEGP 1 (1897), 334-337.

A. S. Cook, "Bemerkungen zu Cynewulfs Crist," *Philologische Studien (Festgabe für Eduard Sievers)*, Halle, 1896.

P. J. Cosijn, "Anglosaxonica IV," *Beiträge zur Geschichte der deutschen Sprache und Literatur* 23 (1898), 109-130.

Matthias Cremer, *Metrische und sprachliche Untersuchung der altenglischen Gedichte Andreas, Guðlac, Phoenix, Elene, Juliana, Crist*, Bonn, 1888.

S. K. Das, *Cynewulf and the Cynewulf Canon*, Calcutta, 1942.

F. Dietrich, "Cynewulfs Crist," *Zeitschrift für deutsches Altertum* 9 (1853), 193-214. (DIETRICH)

M. M. Dubois, *Les Elements Latins dans la Poesie Religieuse de Cynewulf*, Paris, 1943.

G. H. Gerould, "Studies in the Christ," *Englische Studien* 41 (1910), 1-19.

S. B. Greenfield, "The Theme of Spiritual Exile in Christ I," PQ 32 (1953), 321-328.

S. B. Greenfield, "Of Locks and Keys—Line 19a of the OE Christ," MLN 67 (1952), 238-240.

C. W. M. Grein, "Zur Textkritik der angelsächsischen Dichter," *Germania* 10 (1865), 416-429.

S. B. Hemingway, "Cynewulf's Christ 173-176," MLN 22 (1907), 66-73.

F. Holthausen (Review of Grein-Wülker), *Anglia Beiblatt* 9 (1899), 353-358.

F. Holthausen (Review of Cook), *Literaturblatt* 21 (1901), 369-373.

# BIBLIOGRAPHY

K. Jansen, *Cynewulf Forschung, Bonner Beiblatt zur Anglistik* 24, 1908.
C. W. Kennedy, *Early English Christian Poetry*, New York, 1952.
C. W. Kennedy, *The Earliest English Poetry*, New York, 1943.
Neil Ker (Review of Facsimile), *Medium Aevum* 2 (1933), 224-231.
F. Klaeber (Review of Cook), JEGP 4 (1902), 101-112.
Sherman Kuhn, "A Damaged Passage in the Exeter Book," JEGP 50 (1951), 491-493.
H. Leiding, *Die Sprache der Cynewulfschen Dichtungen*, Göttingen, 1887.
F. J. Mather, "The Cynewulf Question from a metrical point of view," MLN 7 (1892), 193-213.
A. A. May, "A Source for Christ 348-377," MLN 24 (1909), 158-159.
Kenneth Mildenberger, "Unity of Cynewulf's *Christ* in the Light of Iconography," *Speculum* 23 (1948), 426-432.
Samuel Moore, "Source of Christ 416ff.," MLN 29 (1914), 226-227.
Samuel Moore, "The Old English Christ: Is it a unit?", JEGP 14 (1918), 550-567.
Brother Augustine Philip, "The Exeter Scribe and the Unity of the Christ," PMLA 55 (1940), 903-909.
Alfred Rose, *Darstellung der Syntax in Cynewulfs Crist*, Halle, 1890.
G. Sarrazin, "Zur Chronologie und Verfasserfrage angelsächsischer Dichtungen," *Englische Studien* 38 (1907), 145-158.
Claes Schaar, *Critical Studies in the Cynewulf Group*, Lund, 1949. (SCHAAR)
Jacob Schipper, "Zum Codex Exoniensis," *Germania* 19 (1874), 327-338.
F. Schwarz, *Cynewulfs Anteil am Crist, Eine metrische Untersuchen*, Köningsberg, 1905.
Kenneth Sisam, "Cynewulf and his Poetry," *Studies in the History of Old English Literature*, Oxford, 1953.
Kenneth Sisam (Review of Facsimile), RES 10 (1934), 338-342.
Moritz Trautmann, "Der sogenannte Crist," *Anglia* 18 (1896), 383-388.
Moritz Trautmann, *Kynewulf, der Bischof und Dichter, Bonner Beiblatt zur Anglistik* 1, 1898.

GLOSSARY AND WORD INDEX

# glossary and word index

ā, adv., *ever, forever*: IV 31, VIII 17, VIII 58, IX 26, XI 10, XI 28, XI 38.
ābēodan, II, *announce, decree*: abead, pret. 3 sg. VIII 16.
ābūgan, II, *shun, avoid*: abugeð, 3 sg. III 7.
ac, conj., *but*: III 7, IV 25, VI 27, VII 37, IX 71, XII 6.
ācennan, W I, *beget*: acenned, pp. V 6, VIII 5.
ācweðan, V, *speak, utter*: acwæð, pret. 3 sg. IX 42.
æ, f., *law*: gs. VI 11.
æfre, adv., *ever*: IV 3, IV 5, IV 9, V 8, VII 15, VIII 25, IX 37, IX 51.
æfter, prep., *after, according to*: IV 7, IX 48, IX 58.
æfterþon, prep., *according to, after*: VIII 22.
ælc, pro., *any, each*: ælces, gsn. IX 59, ælce, asf. XI 29.
ælde, mp., *men*: elda, gp. IX 37; ældum, dp. XI 29.
ælmihtig, adj., *almighty*: nsm. IX 46, IX 57; vsm. VIII 2; ælmihtges, gsm. XI 18; ælmihtigum, dsm. V 18.
æne, adv., *once*: IX 55.
ænig, pro. or adj., *any*: nsm. VIII 6, VIII 28, IX 37, X 4; nsf. IX 17; ænges, gsm. VII 37; ænigne, asm. VII 15; ænige, asf. VII 21.
ær, adv., *before, formerly*: II 22, II 28, III 14, V 12, VI 32, VIII 39, VIII 45, VIII 56, XII 21; ærest, sup. VI 4, VIII 12, X 8.
ær, conj., *until, before*: IX 41.
ær, prep., *before*: VIII 3.
ærdæg, m., *previous time, olden days*: ærdagum, dp. IV 9.
ærþon, conj., *before*: VIII 25.
æt, prep., *on, at, to*: VI 24, VIII 10, VIII 12, VIII 60, X 19, XII 3.
ætwist, f., *presence, being*: ætwiste, gs. XI 15.
æþele, adj., *noble, splendid*: æðelne, asm. XI 25; æðelan, dsmwk. X 3; æþelan, dsnwk. VIII 55.
æþelīc, adj., *noble*: nsm. IX 34.
æþeling, m., *lord, prince*: vs. VI 29.
āfrēfran, W I, *comfort*: inf. VII 12; afrefre, opt. 3 sg. X 21.
āgan, prp., *possess, have*: inf. VI 30.
āgen, adj., *own*: nsn. V 9.
āgend, m., *ruler*: ns. XII 5.
āhreddan, W I, *save, deliver*: inf. I 16; ahredde, pret. 3 sg. II 17; ahredde, opt. 2 sg. X 27.
ālǣtan, VII, *leave, reject*: inf. V 4.
alwalda, m., *ruler of all*: alwaldan, gs. VI 11.
alwiht, n., *every creature*: alwihta, gp. VIII 61, XI 33.

{ 111 }

ān, num., *one, alone*: anum, dsm. VI 24, X 19; ane, npf. III 3; ana, nsf. IX 13.
anginn, n., *beginning*: anginne, ds. V 8.
ānmōdlīce, adv., *unanimously, singlemindedly*: IX 66.
ār, f., *mercy, grace*: are, gs. III 21; are, as. IX 61; arna, gp. VIII 42.
āreccan, W 1, *explain, interpret*: inf. VIII 9, VIII 34; arece, imp. sg. IV 4.
ārfæst, adj., *gracious, good, true*: nsm. VIII 32.
ārian, W.2, *spare, pity*: ara, imp. sg. X 23.
ārīsan, I, *arise*: inf. VIII 54.
āsecgan, W 3, *say, explain*: inf. VIII 8.
āstyrfan, W 1, *kill*: astyrfed, pp. VII 29.
āwæcnan, W 1, *waken, be born*: awæcned, pp. III 18.
āweorpan, III, *cast off, turn away*: aworpen, pp. IV 28.
āwyrgd, pp., *accursed, damned*: awyrda, nsmwk. VIII 43; awyrgde (as noun) apm, VI 29.
bæm, see bēgen.
bēaghroden, adj., *jewel-adorned*: nsf. IX 18.
bealofull, adj. as noun, *enemy, the hostile one*: bealofulla, nsmwk. VIII 46.
bealorāp, m., *dire rope*: bealorapum, ip. X 18.
bealu, n., *evil, bale, affliction*: bealwa, gp. VII 19.
bearn, n., *child, son*: ns. III 17, V 23, VI 18; vs. VII 1; bearnes, gs. II 21, IV 6; as. VII 42, IX 67; bearn, np. IV 16; bearnum, dp. VIII 29.
beclȳsan, W 1, *close, fasten*: beclysed, pp. IX 49.
befōn, r., *receive*: befenge, pret. 2 sg. IV 10.
bēgen, adj., *both*: bæm, dpm. IV 30, X 10.
behindan, prep., *behind*: VI 26.
bemurnan, III, *bemoan, lament*: bemurnest, 2 sg. VII 13.
bend, f., *bond, fetter*: benda, ap. III 19; bendum, dp. VI 18.
bēon (wesan), an., *be, exist*: inf. VII 50; eam, 1 sg. VII 4, VII 43; eart, 2 sg. I 2, III 9, VIII 26, IX 54, XI 26, XI 30; bist, 2 sg. III 8, XI 27; is, 3 sg. I 11, I 13, III 17, IV 18, IV 27, IV 28, IV 29, VI 4, etc.; nis, IV 24, VIII 6, VIII 28; sind, 1 pl. X 15; wære, 2 sg. pret. V 8, VI 2, VIII 3, VIII 23, X 2, X 8; wæs, 3 sg. pret. V 18, V 21, VI 11, VI 13, VIII 11, VIII 15, etc.; næs, X 4; sie, opt. 2 sg. VII 17, IX 6, IX 10; sie, opt. 3 sg. I 4, VIII 17, XI 33, XI 37; wære, opt. pret. 3 sg. IX 30.
beorht, adj., *bright*: nsn. XI 35; beorhtne, asm. VII 42; beorhtan, asfwk. V 10, IX 18; beorhtast, sup. V 1.

## GLOSSARY AND WORD INDEX

beorn, m., *man*: beornum, dp. XI 35.
berēafian, W 2, *bereave, despoil*: bereafod, pp. VII 5.
bescyrian, W 1, *deprive, separate*: bescyrede, pp. npm., II 15.
betlīcast, adj. sup., *best, most excellent*: vsf. III 17.
beþeccan, W 1, *cover, benight*: beþeahte, pp. npm. V 13.
bewindan, III, *encompass, surround, wind around*: bewinde, opt. 3 sg. II 12.
bewrīðan, I, *encompass, wind around*: bewriþen, pp. IX 36.
bī, prep., *by, because of, about, according to*: V 25, VI 5, VII 49, IX 27.
bīdan, I, *await, bide*: bidon, pret. 3 pl. VI 18.
biddan, V, *pray, beg*: bideð, 3 sg. V 10; biddað, 1 pl. VIII 49, X 12; biddað, 3 pl. IX 63.
bifealdan, r., *enfold, wrap*: bifealdne, pp. npm. V 14.
bigong, m., *passage, elapsing* (of time): as. VIII 22.
bihelan, IV, *conceal, hide*: biholen, pp. II 28.
bilūcan, II, *lock, shut*: bileac, pret. 3 sg. IX 60; bilocen, pp. VIII 39.
biter, adj., *bitter*: bitrum, dpm. VI 23.
biwitian, W 2, *take care of, watch over*: biwitigað, 3 pl. X 6.
blētsung, f., *blessing*: ns. IV 30.
bliss, f., *bliss*: blisse, as. III 19.
blīþe, adj., *glad, blithe*: blīþe, isn. IX 6.
blōd, n., *blood*: blode, is. VIII 46.
bona, m., *bane, murderer*: ns. VIII 51.
bōsm, m., *bosom*: bosme, ds. IV 14.
bōt, f., *remedy, relief*: ns. VI 23, X 18.
brād, adj., *broad, wide*: brade, apm. X 10.
brāde, adv., *widely*: XI 3.
brego, m., *lord, protector*: vs. XI 26.
brēman, W 1, *celebrate, honor*: bremende, part. npm. XI 10.
brēostgehygd, f., *inner thoughts, deepest inclinations*: breostgehygdum, dp. VIII 49.
bringan, W 1, *bring*: bringeð, 3 sg. III 19; brohtes, pret. 2 sg. IX 15; brohte, pret. 3 sg. IX 62; bring, imp. sg. VI 21; brungen, pp. V 17.
bringend, m., *bringer*: ns. VI 11.
brūcan, II, *enjoy*: inf. XI 15.
brȳd, f., *bride, woman*: ns. II 21, IX 6, IX 18.
brynetēar, m., *burning tear*: brynetearum, dp. VI 23.
brytengrund, m., *spacious earth*: ap. X 10.
brytenwong, m., *spacious field, surface of earth*: brytenwongas, ap. XI 3.

## GLOSSARY AND WORD INDEX

brytta, m., *lord, giver*: brytta, ns. IX 60; bryttan, gs. IX 7.
burg, f., *city*: burga, gp. III 17.
burglond, n., *homeland, native city*: vs. III 2.
burgsittend, m., *city dweller, human being*: burgsittende, np. IX 63.
būtan, prep., *but, without, except*: II 20, V 8, V 22, VII 44, VIII 58, IX 16, XI 38, XII 24.
būtan, conj., *unless*: VIII 59.
byldo, f., *confidence*: as. V 10.
byrdscipe, m., *pregnancy*: byrdscypes, gs. VII 19.
carcern, n., *prison*: carcerne, ds. II 8.
cearful, adj., *sad, full of care*: cearfulra, gp. II 8.
cearig, adj., used as noun, *miserable, full of care*: cearigum, dp. VI 19.
cearian, W 2, *grieve, be disturbed*: cearigende, part. nsm. VII 14.
ceasterhlid, n., *city gate*: ceasterhlides, gs. IX 40.
cennan, W 1, *bear, bring forth*: inf. IX 24; cennað, 3 pl. IV 17; cende, pp. npm. VIII 19.
cīld, n., *child*: ns. VIII 5.
clǣne, adj., *clean, pure*: clǣne, asf. VII 24, IX 24, IX 57; clǣnan, asmwk. VI 7; clǣneste, sup. nsfwk. IX 2.
cleopian, W 2, *cry out, call*: cleopast, 2 sg. VII 14.
clūstor, n., *lock*: as. IX 40.
cnēoris, f., *generation, race*: cneorissum, dp. VIII 19.
cræft, m., *skill, power*: ns. XII 6, as. VIII 5.
cræftga, m., *craftsman, maker*: ns. I 12.
crīst, m., *Christ*: ns. IV 25, IX 57, XI 14; vs. VI 28, VIII 2, VIII 37, X 11; cristes, gs. III 2, III 16, IX 9.
culpe, f.?, *guilt, fault*: culpan, as. VII 14.
cuman, IV, *come*: inf. VIII 54; cymeð, 3 sg. III 13; cume, opt. 3 sg. I 12; cyme, opt. 2 sg. V 11; cwom, pret. 3 sg. II 29, IV 4, IX 16, XII 5, XII 21; cwome, pret. 2 sg. XI 36; cwome, opt. pret. 3 sg. VI 19; cum, imp. sg. VI 20, VIII 30; cym, imp. sg. X 25; cymen, pp. III 17.
cunnan, prp., *know*: inf. VIII 33; conn, 1 sg. VII 35; conn, 3 sg. III 20; cuðes, pret. 2 sg. IV 7; cuþe, pret. 3 sg. XII 4; cuþan, pret. 3 pl. XII 7.
cūð, adj., *known, understood*: nsn. IV 25, VII 22.
cwealm, m., *death*: cwealme, ds. IV 17.
cwēn, f., *queen*: vs. IX 2.
cweðan, V, *say*: cweþað, 3 pl. IX 9, XI 24; cwæð, pret. 3 sg. IV 17; cwædon, pret. 3 pl. III 16, VI 19; cweden, pp. VII 48.
cynelīce, adv., *royally*: VI 28.

{ 114 }

## GLOSSARY AND WORD INDEX

cynestōl, m., *royal seat*: cynestola, gp. III 2.
cyning, m., *king*: ns. I 12, III 12; vs. II 1, VIII 2, X 25; as. VI 7; cyninges, gs. VII 2; cyninge, ds. I 1, XI 14; cyninga, gp. VI 7, VIII 2.
cynn, n., *race, kind*: ns. XI 9; np. VIII 11; cynne, ds. XII 10.
cyrran, W 1, *turn, go*: cyrre, opt. 2 sg. VI 26.
cyst, m., *best, that which is chosen, excellent*: vs. III 2; as. XI 14.
cȳðan, W 1, *make known, reveal, announce*: inf. IX 23; cyðe, opt. 2 sg. IX 64; cyðdon, pret. 3 pl. III 16.
dǣd, f., *deed*: dædum, dp. XII 14.
dǣdhwæt, adj., *bold, brave in deeds*: dædhwæte, npm. XI 8.
dǣdscūa, m., *deed-shadow, dark deed*: dædscuan, gs. VIII 44.
dǣlan, W 1, *give*: dæleð, 3 sg. XII 13.
dāuīd, m., *David*: dauides, gs. IV 26, VII 2, VII 28.
dēaþ, m., *death*: deaþes, gs. V 15.
dēaðdenu, f., *death valley*: deaðdene, ds. IX 70.
dēgol, adj., *secret, obscure*: nsn. II 24.
dēope, adv., *deeply*: VII 5.
dēor, n., *beast, animal*: ns. VIII 44.
dēore, adj., *precious, dear*: deoran, is. IX 35.
deorc, adj., *dark*: asf. V 15.
dōgor, m., *day*: dogra, gp. XII 13.
dohtor, f., *daughter, descendant*: ns. VII 28; vp. IV 21.
dōm, m., *fate, judgement, fame, honor, glory*: dom, ns. XI 28; domes, gs. VIII 15: dome, is. VII 5, XI 8.
dōmhwæt, adj., *zealous for glory*: domhwate, npm. XII 14.
dōn, anom., *do, make*: dyde, pret. 3 sg. I 17.
drēam, m., *joy, bliss*: dreame, ds. IV 32.
drēogan, II, *suffer, endure*: inf. V 15, VIII 58.
dryhten, m., *Lord*: ns. XII 13; vs. VIII 44, VIII 59, X 1, X 19; dryhtnes, gs. II 24, VII 23, IX 25, XI 19, XI 36; dryhtna, gp. XI 28.
dryhtlīce, adv., *divinely, in a lordly manner*: VIII 15.
dugan, prp., *to avail, to be of value*: deag, 3 sg. II 4, VII 26.
duguþ, f., *men, group of men*: dugeþum, dp. XI 36.
duru, f., *door, gate*: ns. IX 35.
dȳre, adj., *beloved*: dyrre, dsf. IV 26.
ēac, adv., *also, too*: IV 23, VI 7, VI 16, IX 8, IX 27.
ēacen, adj., *increased, magnified, great*: nsf. II 21, asn. VII 42.
ēacnung, f., *increase, conception*: eacnunge, as. IV 5.
ēaden, pp. as adj., *granted, allowed*: VII 37.
ēadig, adj., *blessed*: eadge, nsfwk. IV 17; eadgan, apmwk. II 3.

{ 115 }

ēage, n., *eye*: eagna, gp. I 7; eagum, dp. IX 53, XI 15.
ēala, interjection, *oh, lo*: II 1, III 1, IV 1, V 1, VI 1, VII 1, VII 12, VIII 1, IX 1, X 1, XI 1, XII 1.
ealddagas, mp., *old days, times past*: dp. IX 29.
ealdor, n., *leader, king*: ns. VIII 16; as. I 8.
eal, adv., *completely*: IV 27, VI 24, IX 31, IX 34; eall, X 19.
eall, adj., *all*: eal, nsf. II 25; ealne, asm. IV 2, XII 24; ealle, asf. VII 45, VIII 27; ealle, isn. XI 5; eall, npn. I 7; eal, npn. IV 15; ealle, npm. IX 4, IX 66, X 12, XII 7; ealle, apm. IX 7; ealra, gp. VI 7, VIII 2, IX 13, XI 25; eallum, dp. VIII 3, VIII 32.
eard, m., *home, habitation*: as. III 14.
eardian, W 2, *dwell*: eardað, 3 sg. XII 23; eardedon, pret. 3 pl. V 22.
eardgeard, m., *dwelling, homestead*: eardgearde, ds. III 6.
ēarendel, n., *brightness (Day Star?)*: vs. V 1.
earm, adj., *poor, miserable*: earme, npf. XI 5; earme, apm. I 17; wk. m. as noun, earma, ns. III 21.
ēaþe, adv., *easily*: VII 10.
ēaðmēdu, f., *humility, kindness*: eaðmedu, np. X 12.
ēaðmōd, adj., *humble, meek*: nsm. VIII 42.
ēawan, W 1, *be visible, manifest*: eawed, pp. III 6.
ebrēas, mpl., *Hebrews*: ebrea, gp. III 18.
ebrēsc, adj., *Hebrew*: asn. VI 4.
ēce, adv., *always, eternally*: IX 48.
ēce, adj., *eternal*: ece, nsf. XI 34, XI 38; ece, vsm. VIII 59, X 19; eces, gsm. VI 11; ecan, gsmwk. XI 19; ecan, dsmwk, IX 31; ecne, asm. VI 30, VII 46; ecan, asmwk. X 8.
ēcness, f., *eternity*: ecnesse, ds. IX 39.
efeneardigende, part., *co-existing*: nsm. VIII 24.
efenēce, adj., *coeternal*: nsm. V 19.
efenlīc, adj., *similar, equal*: nsf. II 22.
efenwesende, part., *coeternal*: X 3.
efne, adv., *still, nevertheless, even*: IX 26, IX 56, XII 21.
eft, adv., *again, later, subsequently*: IV 16, V 19, VI 4, IX 51, IX 59.
egesa, m., *terror*: egsan, ds. I 17.
emmānūhēl, m., *Emmanuel*: as. VI 3.
ende, m., *end*: ds. VIII 58, XI 38, XII 24.
ēnga (ānga?) adj., *sole, unique, own?*: engan, asmwk. VIII 24.
enge, adj., *narrow*: asn. II 15.
engel, m., *angel*: engel, ns. VI 3, IX 41, IX 61, X 4; engla gp. III 3, IV 32, V 1, IX 58; englum, dp. XI 10.

eorl, m., *man*: ns. VIII 6.
eorðbūend, m., *earth-dweller*: np. XII 7.
eorðe, f., *earth*: eorðan, ds. VIII 42, IX 2, XI 34; eorðan, as. IX 55.
eorðlīc, adj., *earthly, on earth*: nsm. XI 29.
eorðwaru, f., *earth-dweller*: eorðware, np. XI 5.
eorðburg, f., *earthly city, habitation*: eorðbyrg, as. I 7.
ēowde, n., *flock, herd*: as. VIII 44.
ermðu, f., *misery, wretchedness*: as. VIII 58; yrmþa, ap. X 23.
ēsaīas, m., *Isaiah*: ns. IX 29.
ēðel, m., *native land, country*: eðle, ds. II 15, XII 21.
ēþelstōl, m., *home, native seat*: vs. III 3.
ēua, f., *Eve*: euan, gs. IV 27.
fācen, n., *evil, deceit*: facne, ds. VII 44.
fæder, m., *father*: ns. VII 48, IX 46; gs. V 7, IX 71; ds. V 18; as. VI 34, X 2.
fædrencynn, n., *paternal kin*: as. VIII 35.
fægre, adv., *fairly, beautifully*: XI 13.
fǣhþo, indec. f., *feud, enmity*: as. X 21.
fǣmne, f., *virgin, female*: vs. IV 2, VII 12; ns. II 18, V 20, VII 32, VII 48; fǣmnan, gs. IV 22; fǣmnan, as. VII 24; fǣmnan, ds. XII 3.
fæst, adj., *firm, fast*: fæste, asf. VII 3; fæste, isn. I 6; fæstan, apnwk. IX 47.
fæstlīc, adj., *firm, strong*: apm. IX 38.
fēasceaft, adj., *miserable*: feasceaftne, asm. VII 12; feasceafte, apm. X 21.
fela, indec., *much, many*: II 26, VII 9, VII 18.
feor, adv., *far*: III 7, XI 13; fier, comp. VIII 35.
feorh, m., *life*: asm. XII 24; feore, ds. VIII 17, IX 3 (idiom tō wīdan fēore, see tō).
fier, see feor.
findan, III, *find*: inf. VII 21.
fīras, mp., *men, human beings*: fira, gp. II 18, VIII 29.
firen, f., *sin, crime, iniquity*: firena, gp. III 7, V 20, VII 18, X 22.
fiðere, n., *wing*: fiþrum, ip. XI 18.
flǣsc, n., *flesh, body*: ns. V 20; as. XII 3.
flint, m., *flint*: as. I 6.
fliht, m., *flight*: flihte, ds. XI 22.
folc, n., *folk, people*: folca, gp. XII 11; folcum, dp. VII 32, VIII 12, IX 64.

folde, f., *earth*: foldan, gs. IV 2, VI 15; foldan, as. IX 5, IX 47, XI 31.
folgoð, m., *service, employment, condition of life*: folgoða gp. XI 13.
for, prep., *for*: II 5, V 9, VII 6.
foran, prep., *upon, before*: IX 67.
forcuman, IV, *overcome*: forcymenum, pp. dpm. VI 22.
forescyttels, m., *bolt*: forescyttelsas, ap. IX 38.
forgiefan, V, *grant*: forgeaf, pret. 3 sg. XI 14.
forgifness, f., *forgiveness, mercy, grace*: forgifnesse, as. XII 12.
forgildan, III, *give*: forgildeð, 3 sg. XII 19.
forhwyrfan, W I, *pervert, deprave*: forhwyrfed, pp. II 17.
forlætan, VII, *leave*: forlet, pret. 3 sg. II 13; forlæt, imp. sg. I 10, VII 45.
forpyndan, W I, *dam up, nullify*: forpynded, pp. IV 27.
fortēon, II, *draw away, pull down, seduce*: forteah, pret. 3 sg. VIII 57.
fortyllan, W I, *seize, grasp*: fortylde, pret. 3 sg. VIII 57.
forð, adv., *forth, henceforth, forward*: IV 31, VII 48, VIII 17, IX 25, X 28.
forðgongende, part., *issuing, going forth, continuing*: XII 11.
forþon, adv., *for, therefore, indeed*: II 16, VI 19, VII 6, VIII 28, VIII 48, IX 12, IX 20, XI 8, XI 31, XII 14; forþan, IV 24.
forwyrnan, W I, *refuse, deny*: forwyrneð, 3 sg. II 3.
fracoð, adj., *evil, wicked, abominable*: nsm. VII 32.
frēa, m., *Lord*: frea, ns. IX 54; frea, vs. XI 27; frean, gs. XI 18; frean, as. VIII 24, X 8.
frēobearn, n., *noble son*: freobearne, ds. VIII 10.
frēod, f., *affection*: freode, as. VII 3.
frēolīcast, sup. adj., *noblest*: vsf. IV 2.
frēolīce, adv., *freely, voluntarily*: VII 24.
fricgan, V, *ask*: fricgað, 2 pl. IV 22.
frīgu?, f.?, *embrace, affection*: friga, gp. XII 4; frigum dp. II 20.
frōd, adj., *old and wise*: nsmwk. IX 52.
friðgeard, n., *home of peace*: friðgeardum, dp. XI 22.
frōfor, f., *comfort*: frofre, gs. VII 44; frofre, ds. III 16; frofre, as. IX 64.
from, prep., *from*: I 17.
fromcyn, n., *origin, descent*: as. VIII 29.
fruma, m., *originator, creator*: ns. IX 20; fruman, ds. II 27.
fruma, m., *beginning*: fruman, ds. VIII 12.
frumcyn, n., *race*: II 18.

frymð, f., *beginning*: frymðe, ds. V 18, VIII 10.
ful, adv., *full, very*: VIII 39, XI 12.
full, adj., *full*: ns. III 8, IV 17, XI 1.
fyrwet, n., *curiosity*: fyrwet, as. IV 22.
gabriēl, m., *Gabriel*: ns. IX 62; gabrihel, ns. VII 38.
gǣst, m., *soul, spirit*: gæst, ns. VII 40, VII 44, VIII 56; gæstes, gs. VI 16, IX 45; gæste, ds. VI 10; gæstas np. X 16; gæsta, gp. VI 1, VII 33.
gǣstlīc, adj., *spiritual*: ns. II 25.
gē, pro., *ye, you*: np. IV 19.
geard, n., *home, yard*: geardum, dp. VII 38.
gēardagas, mp., *days of yore, past times*: geardagum, dp. VIII 38.
gearnung, f., *merit, earning*: ns. II 23 (mistake for geearnung? cf. geacnod, *Elene* 341).
gēaro, adv., *of old, formerly, long ago*: V 6 (cf. Bede, Sch. 552, 30).
geat, n., *gate*: geatu, ap. VIII 38; gatu, ap. IX 44.
gebedscipe, m., *sexual intercourse*: as. IV 6.
geberan, IV, *bear*: inf. VII 42; gebære, pret. 2 sg. IV 14; gebær, pret. 3 sg. V 20.
gebētan, W 1, *improve, better*: gebete, opt. 3 sg. I 13.
gebīdan, I, *await*: inf. III 21.
gebindan, III, *bind, fasten, encrust*: gebunden, pp. IX 34, X 18.
geblētsian, W 2, *bless*: gebletsad, pp. XI 35.
geblissian, W 2, *bless*: geblissa, imp. sg. VIII 36; geblissad, pp. XI 3.
gebodian, W 2, *bid, say, announce*: gebodade, pret. 3 sg. VII 39.
gebrosnian, W 2, *corrupt, defile*: gebrosnad, pp. I 13, IV 14.
gebycgan, W 1, *buy*: gebohtes, pret. 2 sg. VIII 46.
gebyrd, fn., *birth, childbearing*: as. II 21, III 16, IX 24; gebyrde, as. IV 6.
gecēosan, II, *select, choose*: geceas, pret. 3 sg. II 19; gecorene, pp. asf. IX 57.
gecweðan, V, *speak*: gecwæð, pret. 3 sg. VI 3.
gecȳðan, W 1, *show, manifest*; gecyð, imp. sg. VI 28.
gedǣlan, W 1, *separate, sever from*: inf. VII 3; gedælde, pret. 3 sg. VIII 15.
gedōn, anom., *make, do*: gedo, opt. 3 sg. II 13.
gedrēfan, W 1, *trouble, disturb*: gedrefed, pp. VII 5.
gedrēosan, II, *fall*: gedreose, opt. 3 sg. VIII 52.
gedwola, m., *error, sin*: gedwolan, as. IX 70.
geeardian, W 2, *dwell*: geeardode, pret. 3 sg. VII 45.
gefǣlsian, W 2, *purify*: VI 15.

## GLOSSARY AND WORD INDEX

gefælsian, W 2, *pass through*: IX 46.

gefēa, m., *comfort, joy*: ns. VIII 18; as. VI 30.

geferian, W 1, *carry, take*: geferge, opt. 3 sg. IX 71.

gefōg, n., *joining, union*: gefoge, is. I 6.

gefremman, W 1, *do, make*: gefremme, opt. 2 sg. VIII 50; gefremede, pret. 3 sg. XII 9; gefremed, pp. VII 44, X 22.

gefrignan, III, *learn by inquiry, hear*: gefrugnen, opt. 3 pl. VIII 12; gefrugnon, pret. 1 pl. IX 27; gefrugnan, pret. 1 pl. IV 8.

gefyllan, W 1, *fill, fulfill*: gefyldest, pret. 2 sg. XI 31; gefylled, pp. VII 18, VII 50, IX 52.

gefyrn, adv., *formerly, of old, long ago*: III 14, VI 6, IX 27, X 2.

gehǣlan, W 1, *heal, comfort*: inf. VII 11.

gehālgod, pp. adj., *holy, blessed*: gehalgoda, nsmwk. XII 20.

gehātan, VII, *call, name, promise*: gehaten, pp. III 9, VI 13.

gehealdan, VII, *keep, hold*: inf. IX 26; geheold, pret. 1 sg. IV 23.

gehroden, pp. adj., *adorned, furnished*: gehrodene, asf. IX 56.

gehþu, f., *grief, affliction*: gehþum, dp. IV 20.

gehwā, indef. pro., *each*: gehwǣs, gsn. II 30; gehwam, dsm. VII 31, VIII 18, XII 13; gehwone, asm. III 12; gehwane, asf. V 4.

gehwylc, pro., *each, whatever*: nsm. III 7; gehwylcre, gsf. VII 17; gehwylcum, dsm. XII 16.

gehwyrfan, W 1, *overthrow, change*: gehwyrfed, pp. VII 25.

gehȳran, W 1, *hear*: gehyre, opt. 2 sg. X 13; gehyred, pp. VII 8.

gehyrst, pp. adj., *adorned*: gehyrste, npm. XI 16.

gelǣdan, W 1, *guide, lead*: gelǣded, pp. IX 30.

gelimpan, III, *occur, happen*: inf. IV 9; gelomp, pret. 3 sg. VIII 20.

gelong, adj., *pertaining to, dependent on*: nsf. VI 23, X 18.

gelȳfan, W 1, *believe, expect*: gelyfað, 1 pl. V 16.

gemǣcscipe, m., *coupling, cohabitation*: as. VII 36.

gemǣne, adj., *joint, common*: nsm. X 10; nsf. IV 30.

gemētan, W 1, *find*: gemette, pret. 3 sg. IX 56.

gemiclian, W 2, *magnify, glorify*: gemiclað, 3 sg. II 30.

gemynd, n., *mind, intelligence, memory*: as. XII 16.

gēn, adv., *yet, still*: VII 29, VII 35.

geneahhe, adv., *wholly, fully*: II 31.

genēdan, W 1, *force, impose*: genedde (MS geneðde) pp. apm. III 20.

geniman, IV, *take*: genom, pret. 3 sg. VIII 10.

genyrwian, W 2, *oppress*: genyrwad, pp. X 17.

gēoc, f., *help, aid*: geoce, ds. V 21.

gēocend, m., *savior*: as. VII 35.

gēomor, adj., *miserable, sorrowful*: geomrum, dpm. V 21.
gēomormōd, adj., *sorrowful in mind*: nsm. VII 10.
gēomrian, W 2, *sorrow, lament*: geomrende, part. npm. IV 20.
geond, prep., *through, throughout*: I 7, III 10, IV 1, IX 5, IX 32, XI 3.
geondsprūtan, II, *sprout around, pervade*: geondspreot (for spreat?) pret. 3 sg. II 25.
geondwlītan, I, *look around, survey*: geondwlite (MS geondwlitan) opt. 2 sg. III 11.
geong, adj., *young*: vsf. VII 12; nsf. II 18; geongre, dsf. VII 38.
georne, adv., *eagerly*: XI 20.
geornlīce, adv., *earnestly, eagerly*: VIII 49; geornlicost, sup. XII 18.
gēotan, II, *fall, drop, shed*: inf. VII 10.
gereccan, W 1, *interpret*: gereht, pp. VI 4.
gerestan, W 1, *rest, abide*: gerestað, 3 pl. III 4.
gerīsan, I, *to become, befit, suit*: geriseð, 3 sg. I 3.
gerȳne, n., *secret, mystery, miracle, hidden meaning*: ns. II 24, IV 25; as. IV 4, XII 8; gerynum, dp. VI 5.
gesǣlig, adj., *blessed*: nsm. XII 23.
gesceaft, f., *creation*: as. III 10, VIII 26, X 9; gesceafta, gp. XI 25.
gescyppan, VI, *create, make*: gescop, pret. 3 sg. I 14, II 6.
gesēcan, W 1, *seek*: inf. VI 17; geseceð, 3 sg. III 13; gesece, imp. sg. VIII 41.
gesēþan, W 1, *prove, state as true*: inf. VIII 30.
gesihð, f., *sight*: vs. III 1; gesihþe, ds. I 7.
gesleccan, W 1, *weaken, enfeeble*: geslæhte, pp. npm. VI 20.
gesomnigan, W 2, *bring together, gather*: gesomnige, opt. 2 sg. I 5.
gestarian, W 2, *spy, see*: gestarode, pret. 3 sg. IX 33.
gestaðelian, W 2, *establish, fix*: gestaþelad, pp. IX 33.
gesteald, n. *place, location, dwelling*: as. IX 30.
gesweotulian, W 2, *reveal, make clear*: gesweotula, imp. sg. I 9.
geswenct, pp. adj., *harassed, belabored*: geswencte, npm. X 15.
geswīðde, pp. adj., *confirmed, honored*: nsm. XI 8.
geþencan, W 1, *consider, think, resolve*: geþohtest, pret. 2 sg. IX 14; geþence, imp. sg. X 23.
geþēon, W 1, *do, accomplish*: X 30.
geþingian, W 2, *intercede, mediate*: geþinga, imp. sg. IX 68.
geþonc, m., *thought*: as. IX 41.
geþwǣre, adj., *united, harmonious*: npm. V 24.
geweald, n., *rule, dominion*: ns. VIII 15.
geweorc, n., *work*: ns. V 9.

geweorðan, III, *be, become, occur*: gewearð, pret. 1 sg. IV 23, VII
47; gewearð, pret. 3 sg. II 23, IX 43, V 19; gewurde, pret.
opt. 3 sg. VIII 25, IX 3; geworden, pp. II 20, VIII 3, VIII 13,
VIII 17, X 4.
geweorþian, W 2, *honor, praise*: geweorþad, pp. XI 30.
gewill, n., *will, wishes*: as. X 15.
gewin, n., *struggle, strife*: gewinnes, gs. III 8.
gewitt, n., *wit, mind*: as. II 12.
gewuldrian, W 2, *glorify*: gewuldrad, pp. IV 28.
gewyrcan, W 1, *make, do, create*: geworhtes, pret. 2 sg. VI 32;
geworhtra, pp. gp. VII 16 (*accomplished, committed*).
gewyrht, n., *act, deed*: gewyrhtum, dp. V 25.
giefu, f., *gift*: giofu, ns. II 25.
gīet, adv., *yet*: IX 44, X 4.
gif, conj., *if*: II 4, VII 27.
git, dual pro., *you two*: inc, dp. X 10.
glæd, adj., *glad, blithe, happy*: glædne, asm. IX 41.
glēaw, adj., *wise, sagacious*: nsm. VI 10, VIII 7.
glēawlīce, adv., *wisely, aptly*: VI 1.
god, m., *God*: vs. VI 1, VIII 60, X 14; ns. V 6, V 21, VI 6, VII 10,
VIII 13, IX 45, IX 50, XI 6, XI 30; godes, gs. V 17, VI 18,
VII 42, IX 41, IX 61; gode, ds. V 6; god, as. V 19, IX 73,
XII 18.
godþrym, m., *God's glory*: as. VI 10.
gomel, adj., used as noun, *wise man, prophet*: gomele, npm. VI 6.
gong, n., *going, journey*: as. VIII 41.
grund, m., *the abyss, hell*: as. VIII 52; grundas, ap. VI 16.
grundscēat, m., *surface of the earth*: as. II 25.
guma, m., *man*: gumum, dp. XII 12.
gylden, adj., *golden*: gyldnan, apnwk. VIII 38, IX 44.
habban, W 3, *have*: hæbbe, 1 sg. VII 6, VII 18; hafað, 3 sg. VIII
43, XII 16; habbað, 3 pl. X 16, XI 13; habben, opt. 1 pl. X 22.
hād, m., *state, status, manner, sex*: ns. IV 29; as. II 32, IV 22;
hada, gp. IX 12.
hæft, m., *captive, prisoner*: as. VIII 47; hæftas, ap. VI 25; hæfta,
gp. X 13.
hælend, m., *Savior*: vs. X 11; ns. XI 6, XII 20.
hælende, part., *healing, saving*: VIII 37.
hæleþ, m., *man, hero*: np. IX 5; hæleþa, gp. VIII 53, X 25.
hǣlo, indec. f., *health, salvation, greeting*: ns. XI 34; as. V 16, VII
39; gs. VI 21.
hǣlogiefu, f., *gift of salvation*: hǣlogiefe, as. X 27.

hālig, adj., *holy*: nsm. XI 26, XI 27; vsf. XI 2; halga, vsmwk. X 1; halgan, gsmwk. III 9; halgum, dp. IX 10.

hām, m., *home*: ds. IX 31, X 3.

hātan, VII, *command, call, name*: hatað, 3 pl. IX 5; hat, imp. sg. VIII 40; heht, pret. 3 sg. IX 20.

hē, pro., *he*: ns. I 14, II 7, II 13, II 17, II 19, V 26, IX 30, etc.; his, gs. II 4, IV 21, VI 12, VII 43, VII 47, VIII 5, etc.; him, ds. II 19, VII 50, VIII 10, VIII 15, IX 48, IX 58, XI 23; hine, as. V 26, XI 7, XII 14; hie, np. VI 17; hio, IX 48; hy, X 8, XI 15; hy, ap. IX 51; hyra, gp. XI 18, XI 21; him, dp. VI 13, VIII 47, XI 14.

hēafod, n., *head*: heafod (MS heafoð) ns. I 4.

hēah, adj., *high, exalted*: nsf. XI 2.

hēahboda, m., *high messenger*: heahbodan, as. IX 21.

hēahcyning, m., *High King*: vsm. VI 21.

hēahengel, m., *archangel*: heagengel, ns. VII 39; heahengla, gp. XI 26.

hēahfrēa, m., *High Lord*: ns. XII 9; vs. VIII 40.

hēahgǣst, m., *Holy Ghost*: ns. X 11.

hēahlīc, adj., *noble, sublime*: healic, nsm. XII 15.

hēahlīce, adv., *exaltedly*: XI 6, XI 12.

hēahþu, f., *height, highest*: heahþum, dp. XI 27.

healdan, VII, *hold, keep*: healdeð, 3 sg. II 2.

healf, f., *side, half*: healfa, gp. III 12.

heall, f., *hall, temple*: healle, gs. I 4.

hēan, adj., *mean, inferior, humble*: nsm. VIII 52; heanum, dpm. XI 37; heanra, comp. nsm. IV 29.

hēanlīce, adv., *miserably, abjectly*: II 14, X 25.

hēanniss, f., *heights, exaltation*: heannissum, dp. VI 33; heannessum, dp. XI 33.

hēap, m., *crowd, group*: as. I 16.

hearde, adv., *severely*: X 17.

heardlīce, adv., *severely*: VIII 47.

hearm, m., *harm, insult*: hearmes, gs. VII 8.

helan, IV, *conceal, cover up*: hele, opt. 1 sg. VII 30.

hell, f., *hell*: helle, gs. VIII 52.

helm, m., *protector*: vs. VIII 61, XI 33.

help, f., *help, aid*: helpe, ds. XII 12; helpe, as. VIII 50, XII 9.

helpan, III, *help*: help, imp. sg. X 20.

helsceaþa, m., *hell-harmer, devil*: helsceaþan, (MS helsceaþa) np. X 17.

helware, fp., *inhabitants of hell*: helwara, gp. IX 12.

heofon, m., *heaven*: heofones, gs. III 12, VI 21, VII 39; heofona, gp. VIII 40, X 1, XII 9; heofonum, dp. IX 8, IX 12.
heofoncund, adj., *divine, heavenly*: nsf. XI 2.
heofonhām, n., *heavenly home, divine seat*: heofonhame, ds. IX 19.
heonan, adv., *hence*: VI 26.
heorte, f., *heart*: heortan, gs. VII 11.
hēr, adv., *here*: V 13, VIII 11, VIII 31.
hērcyme, m., *advent, coming hither*: as. VII 37.
herenis, f., *praise*: ns. XI 38.
hergan, W 1, *praise*: inf. II 32; XI 6; hergen, opt. 1 pl. XII 15.
hetol, adj., *hateful, hostile*: hetlen (MS hetlen) npm. X 17.
hider, adv., *hither*: VI 25, IX 21.
hidercyme, m., *advent, coming hither*: ns. X 20; as. VI 13.
hierusalem, m., *Jerusalem*: vs. III 1.
hit, pro., *it*: ns. VIII 20; as. III 14, VI 3, XII 7.
hlæfdige, f., *lady*: ns. IX 10.
hlēo, m., *protector*: vs. XI 32.
hlēofæst, adj. *protecting, comforting*: ns. X 11.
hlūd, adv., *loud*: hludan, isfwk. XI 12.
hlūtor, adj., *pure, clear*: hlutre, ds. IX 19.
holdlīce, adv., *faithfully, loyally*: XII 15.
hond, f., *hand*: hondum, dp. VI 33.
hondgeweorc, n., *handiwork*: ns. VIII 53.
horsc, adj., *wise, enlightened*: nsm. VIII 28; horscne (MS hoscne) as. II 32.
hosp, m., *scorn, insult*: as. VII 8.
hoðma, m., *earth, sod*: hoðman, ds. II 28.
hrā (hrǣw), n., *body*: I 14.
hrædlīce, adv., *quickly, immediately*: VIII 50.
hreddan, W 1, *save*: inf. VIII 61.
hrēmig, adj., *exultant*: hremge, npf. III 5.
hrēowcearig, adj., *sorrowful, full of heavy care*: hreowcearigum, dpm. X 20.
hrif, n., *womb*: ds. XII 10; as. XII 10.
hrōf, m., *roof*: hrofe, ds. I 14; as. III 11.
hrōþor, m., *solace, comfort*: hroþre, ds. XI 37.
hū, adv., *how*: III 12, III 21, IV 5, IV 22, VI 1, VII 20, VIII 2, VIII 9, IX 4, X 15, X 24, XII 8.
hūru, adv., *indeed, certainly*: II 5, IV 12, IX 63.
hūs, n., *house*: ns. I 14.
hwæt, inter. pro., *what*: IV 19, VII 13.
hwæt, interjection, *what, lo*: XII 1.

hwearfian, W 2, *wander, roam about*: hwearfiað, 1 pl. X 25.
hweorfan, III, *turn, return, go*: II 14.
hwonne, conj., *when, until*: II 10, VI 18.
hwylc, pro., *which*: nsm. XI 21.
hygecræftig, adj., *intelligent, strong of mind*: nsm. VIII 28.
hygegēomor, adj., *heartsick, sad*: hygegeomre, npm. VI 25.
hygesorg, f., *mental distress*: hygesorge, as. VII 11.
hȳhst, super. adj. as noun, *highest ones*: hyhstan, npm. IX 8 (super. of hēah).
hyht, n., *joy, hope*: ns. IV 29; hyhtes, gs. III 9.
hyhtan, W 1, *wish for, hope*: inf. IX 66; pret. 3 pl. VI 13.
hyhtfull, adj., *hopeful*: hyhtfulle, npm. V 16.
hȳnan, W 1, *humiliate, debase, oppress*: hyneð, 3 sg. VIII 47.
hȳran, W 1, *hear, obey*: inf. IX 70; hyrdon, pret. 3 pl. IV 3.
iācōb, m., *Jacob*: iacobes, gs. VII 1.
ic, pro., *I*: ns. IV 22, VII 4, VII 6, etc.; me, ds. VII 8, VII 26, VII 37, VII 38, etc.
in, prep., *in, on, at*: II 8, II 23, III 3, III 6, III 14, IV 9, IV 10, IV 12, IV 26, IV 32, V 7, etc.
inc, see git.
inca, m., *offence, fault*: incan, as. VII 15.
ingong, m., *gate, entrance*: ns. IX 34.
inlocast, super. adv., *innermost, most profoundly*: XII 17. (See note.)
inhebban, VI, *raise up, lift*: inhebban (MS inhebba) inf. IX 39.
inlēohtan, W 1, *illumine, lighten*: inleohte, opt. 2 sg. V 12.
inlīhtan, W 1, *illumine, lighten*: inlihtes, 2 sg. V 5; inlihted, pp. II 26.
iōsēph, m., *Joseph*: vs. VII 1.
īowan, W 2, *manifest, show*: iowa, imp. sg. IX 61.
īu, adv., *of old, long ago*: I 2, VI 9.
lāc, n., *gift, sacrifice*: ap. IX 18.
lācan, VII, *swing, play, move about*: inf. XI 22.
lādigan, W 1, *refute, defend oneself*: inf. VII 20.
lǣdend, m., *giver, one who introduces*: ns. VI 12.
lǣfan, W 1, *leave, grant*: læf, imp. sg. VI 31.
lǣmen, adj., *made of clay*: læmena, apn. I 15.
lǣtan, VII, *leave, allow*: læte, opt. 3 sg. IX 69; læt, imp. sg. VI 26, VI 29.
lār, f., *knowledge, wisdom*: lare, np. II 27; lara, gp. VI 12.
latian, W 2, *linger, delay*: lata, imp. sg. X 26.
lāþ, adj., *hateful, hostile*: laþ, nsm. VII 31; laþan, gsf. VII 20.

## GLOSSARY AND WORD INDEX

lēan, n., *reward*: as. XII 19.
lēas, adj., *lacking, free from, without*: nsn. V 20; nsf. II 19; lease, asf. VII 25.
lēode, fp., *people, race*: leoda, gp. VII 31, VIII 21.
lēodsceaþa, m., *harmer of people, enemy*: leodsceaþan, ds. VIII 60.
lēoflīc, adj. noun, *dear one*: leoflicne, asm. XI 23.
lēoht, n., *light*: ns. VIII 18; leohte, ds. XI 23; as. II 10, VIII 14.
lēohtian, W 2, *illumine, light*: leohtade, pret. 3 sg. VIII 21.
lēoma, m., *gleam, light, splendor*: ns. VIII 21; vs. V 3; leoman, is. VII 41.
licgan, IV, *lie, be situated*: lægon, pret. 3 pl. II 28.
līf, n., *life*: as. II 2, VI 21; lifes, gs. II 27, VII 41, VIII 14, IX 30, IX 60; life, ds. XII 1.
līffrēa, m., *Lord of Life*: ns. I 15, II 10.
lifgan, W 2, *live*: inf. VII 31; leofa, imp. sg. XI 35; lifgende, part. vs. VIII 60; lifgendra, part. gp. VIII 18, XII 22.
lim, n., *limb*: leomo, ap. I 15.
lioðucæge, f., *key to the body or limbs*: lioðucægan, is. IX 60.
liss, f., *love, mercy, grace*: lisse, gs. XII 19; lissa, gp. X 26.
līxan, W 1, *shine*: lixende, part. nsn. VIII 18.
loc, n., *lock*: locu, ap. IX 47.
loca, m., *lock*: locan, ap. II 2.
lof, m., *praise*: as. XI 34.
lofian, W 2, *praise*: lofiað, 3 pl. XI 23.
lond, n., *land*: as. II 15; londes, gs. XII 22.
longe, adv., *long*: V 12, VI 12, VIII 39; lange, X 26, leng, comp. IX 69.
longsum, adj., *long enduring*: longsume, npf. II 27.
lufu, f., *love*: lufan, as. VII 3.
lungre, adv., *suddenly*: VII 4.
lust, m., *desire, pleasure*: as. VIII 48, X 22.
lyft, f., *sky, air*: lyfte, ds. VIII 6.
mā, adv., *more*: IX 51.
mā, adj., *greater, more*: XII 6.
mæg, f., *maid, virgin*: ns. IV 17.
mæg, f., *descendant, kinsman*: vs. VII 2.
mæge, f., *relative, descendant*: mægan, ds. IV 26.
mægen, n., *power, might*: mægne, ds. VI 16; mægne, is. IX 45; mægene, is. XI 5.
mægenþrym, m., *angelic band*: mægenþrymmes, gs. X 5; mægenþrymme, ds. IX 22.
mægþ, f., *people, race*: mægþe, ap. VI 15; mægþum, dp. VIII 21.

{ 126 }

## GLOSSARY AND WORD INDEX

mægþ, f., *virgin, maid*: ns. II 19; vs. VII 13.
mægþhād, m., *virginity, maidenhood*: ns. IV 15; as. IX 15.
mǣnan, W I, *complain, bemoan*: mænað, 3 pl. IV 20.
mænigo, f. indec., *crowd, multitude*: as. VI 27.
mǣre, adj., *great, glorious*: mæra, vsfwk. IX 1; mæra, nsmwk.
    VI 9; mæran, gsmwk. VII 2; mærre, gsf. I 4; mære, nsf.
    IV 24; mærum, dsm. VII 47.
magan, prp., *be able, may*: mæg, 1 sg. VII 20, IX 43; mæg, 3 sg.
    II 16, VII 10; mæge, opt. 3 sg. VIII 8, VIII 29, XI 21; magon,
    1 pl. V 24; mægon, 1 pl. VIII 34; meahte, pret. 3 sg. IX 37.
mān, n., *sin, iniquity*: manes, gs. II 19.
mānswara, m., *forsworn person, evil doer*: ns. VII 30.
marīa, f., *Mary*: ns. IV 18; vs. VII 13, IX 25.
meaht, f., *might*: as. VIII 5; meahta, gp. IX 22; meahtum, dp. IX
    10, IX 56.
mēdrencynn, n., *maternal lineage*: as. VIII 33.
mēlchisēdech, m., *Melchisedech*: ns. VI 9.
meotod, m., *God*: vs. VIII 31; meotudes, gs. IV 24, V 23,
    VI 14, VII 34; meotodes, gs. VII 47; meotude, ds. IX 15.
micel, adj., *great, large*: micle, asf. VI 27; micla, nsmwk. IV 15;
    miclan, gsmwk. X 5.
mid, prep., *with*: IV 33, V 19, V 21, VI 2, VI 6, VI 34, VIII 4, VIII 9,
    VIII 12, VIII 22, VIII 24, VIII 27, IX 4, etc.
middangeard, m., *world*: middangeardes, gs. IX 1; ds. V 2; as.
    VIII 36.
mihtig, adj., *mighty*: nsn. V 23.
mild, adj., *gentle, mild*: milde, nsm. XII 2.
milde, adv., *mildly, gently*: VIII 36.
milts, f., *mercy, grace*: miltse, ds. IX 25; miltse, as. VI 27, VIII 31.
mīn, poss. pro., *my*: vs. VII 1; minre, gsf. VII 11; mine, asf. VII 4;
    minne, asm. IV 23.
mōd, n., *mind, spirit, way of thinking*: mod, ds. IV 7; mode, ds.
    II 11, IX 6, IX 19, X 24.
mōdor, f., *mother*: ns. IV 23, VII 47; gs. XII 10; meder, ds. II 19.
molde, f., *earth*: moldan, ds. XII 6.
mon, m., *man*: monnes, gs. V 23, VII 36, XII 6; mon, as. II 6;
    manna, gp. IV 15; monna, IX 13, XII 10, XII 16, monnum,
    dp. IV 24, V 2, IX 25; men, ap. IX 17.
moncyn, n., *mankind*: moncynnes, gs. VIII 31, XII 2.
monwīs, adj., *manlike, human*: monwisan, ds. IV 7.
morþor, n., *crime, sin*: as. VII 30.

## GLOSSARY AND WORD INDEX

mōtan, anom., *may, be able, must*: mot, 3 sg. IV 30; motan, 1 pl. VIII 33, IX 65, IX 72, XI 7; moton, 3 pl. XI 15; mote, opt. 3 sg. VIII 54; moten, opt. 1 pl. X 29.
mund, m., *purity?*: as. IV 23.
mundbora, m., *support, protector*: mundboran, ds. II 11.
næfre, adv., *never*: III 5.
nænig, pro., *none, not any*: ns. II 22, IV 50.
næs, nis, see beon.
nān, indef. pro., *none*: IX 16, X 5.
nāthwylc, indef. pro., *some unknown thing, I know not what*: nathwylces, gs. VII 26.
nāwðer, pro., *neither*: nsn. VII 26.
ne, negative adverbial particle, *not, no, nor*: II 4, II 7, II 22, IV 7, IV 8, IV 11, VI 26, VI 29, VII 14, VII 27, etc.
nēah, adv., *near*: XI 13; nehst, sup. XI 21.
nearoþearf, f., *dire need*: nearoþearfe, as. III 20.
nemnan, W 1, *name*: nemned, pp. VI 2.
nēod, f., *wish, desire*: ns. VIII 32; nioda, gp. VIII 48.
nēosan, W 1, *visit*: IX 47.
nergend, m., *savior*: vs. VIII 48; ns. IX 50, XII 11; nergende, ds. XI 21.
nergende, part. adj., *saving*: VI 28, X 14.
nīedþīow, m., *servant, slave*: niedþiowa, gp. X 14.
niman, IV, *take*: nimeð, 3 sg. III 14, VIII 47.
nīþ, m., *iniquity, enmity, malice*: niþum, dp. III 20.
nō, adv., *not, by no means*: IV 14.
noma, m., *name*: noman, as. II 31; noman, ds. VI 2, XI 36.
nū, adv., *now*: I 9, I 11, I 13, I 15, III 10, III 17, IV 13, IV 30, V 9, V 16, V 19, etc.
nymþe, conj., *but, except*: IX 50.
ō, adv., *ever*: IX 39, see ā.
of, prep., *of, from*: IV 4, V 5, V 6, VII 23, IX 21.
ofer, prep., *over, against, beyond, from*: IV 2, V 2, V 4, VI 29, VIII 48, IX 2, IX 17, XII 6.
oferþearf, f., *extreme distress?*: oferþearfum, dp. VI 24.
ofostlīce, adv., *often*: comp. þon ofostlicor, VIII 59.
oft, adv., *often*: I 17; oftost, super. XII 17.
ōht, see ōwihte.
on, adv., *on*: IX 53.
on, prep., *on, in*: V 18, V 24, VI 4, VI 27, VII 37, VIII 47, VIII 54, IX 8, IX 39, IX 55, IX 67, X 30.
onbeht, m., *servant*: onbehtum, dp. X 23.

{ 128 }

## GLOSSARY AND WORD INDEX

ond, conj., *and*: (always abbreviated 7) I 5, I 10, II 1, II 12, III 3, etc.
ondswaru, f., *answer*: ondsware, as. VII 21.
onfindan, III irreg., *find, discover*: onfunde, pret. 1 sg. VII 16.
onfōn, VII, *receive*: onfenge, opt. 2 sg. IV 5; onfeng, pret. 1 sg. VII 24; onfeng, pret. 3 sg. XII 3; onfangen, pp. IV 29; onfongen, pp. VII 19.
onlūcan, II, *unlock, open*: inf. IX 40; onluceð, 3 sg. IX 51.
onlȳhtan, W 1, *illumine, light up*: onlyhte, opt. 3 sg. VII 41.
onlȳsan, W 1, *release, loose*: onlyseð, 3 sg. III 19.
onsendan, W 1, *send*: onsende, opt. 2 sg. V 11.
onsȳn, f., *face, visage*: onsyne, as. XI 19.
ontȳnan, W 1, *open, unlock, reveal*: inf. VIII 40; ontyneð, 3 sg. II 2; ontyne, opt. 3 sg. II 10.
onwald, m., *power, rule*: as. VI 30.
onwrēon, I, *reveal*: onwrah, pret. 3 sg. IV 25, VI 10, VII 32, IX 42, XI 7.
ordfruma, m., *creator, originator*: ns. VIII 14; ordfruman, as. XI 25.
ormǣte, adj., *huge, immense*: nsf. IX 33.
ōþer, pro., *other, second one*: nsf. IX 17; nsm. IX 50; oþrum, dpm. II 3.
oþþæt, conj., *until*: IX 33.
oþþe, conj., *or*: VII 21, IX 40.
ōwer, adv., *ever, at any time*: VII 36.
ōwiht, pro., *aught, any, a bit*: oht, ns. VIII 25; owihte, is. VIII 35, IX 69.

rǣd, m., *counsel, course of action*: ns. XII 15.
reccend, m., *Lord*: II 1.
reord, f., *voice, spoken word*: reorda, gp. II 30.
reordberend, m., *possessors of speech, creatures capable of speech*: np. IX 4; reordberende, np. XI 4.
reordian, W 2, *speak*: reordode, pret. 3 sg. VII 33.
rīce, n., *kingdom*: ds. VIII 55; as. IX 71, X 6.
rīpan, I, *reap*: ripað, 3 pl. IV 16.
rodor, m., *heaven, sky*: rodores, gs. III 11; rodoras, ap. XI 31; rodera, gp. VI 5, VIII 9, XII 8; roderum, dp. IV 4, X 6.
rūme, adv., *widely, clearly*: III 11, VI 4.
riht, adj., *right, true*: vsm. II 1.
ryht, n., *right, truth*: as. VIII 54; ryhte, ds. VIII 9, IX 4, XI 4.
ryhte, adv., *rightly*: VI 2.

## GLOSSARY AND WORD INDEX

ryhtgerȳne, n., *miracle, obscure meaning*: ryhtgeryno, ap. VII 33, VIII 34.
rȳne, n., *obscure meaning, mystery*: as. II 30.
sācerd, m., *priest*: as. VI 8.
sǣd, n., *seed*: as. XII 5.
sancta, adj., *holy, saint*: s̄c̄a, vsf. III 1; ns. IV 18.
sār, adj., *sore, sorrowful*: sare, asf. VII 46.
sārcwide, m., *bitter words, injurious speech*: sarcwida, gp. VII 7.
sāwan, VII, *sow*: sawað, 3 pl. IV 16.
sāwol, f., *soul*: saule, np. III 4.
sceadu, f., *shadow*: as. V 15.
scēat, m., *surface*: as. IV 2.
scēawian, W 2, *look at, view*: sceawode, pret. 3 sg. IX 31.
sculan, prp., *must, ought, shall*: sceal, 1 sg. VII 9; scealt, 2 sg. VII 3; sceal, 3 sg. I 15, III 21, VII 28; sculon, 1 pl. VIII 58; sculon, 3 pl. XI 4; scyle, opt. 1 sg. VII 30; sceolde, pret. 1 sg. VII 41; sceolde, pret. 3 sg. VII 49, VIII 20; sceoldan, pret. 1 pl. II 14; sceoldan, pret. 3 pl. V 15; sceolde, opt. pret. 2 sg. IX 24.
scyld, f., *guilt*: ns. IV 27.
scyppend, m., *Creator*: vs. VIII 53: ns. XII 2; scyppendes, gs. II 31.
sē, se, dem. pro., and article, *the, that, he*, etc.: nsm. I 2, I 12, II 29, III 21, IV 15, etc.; þæs, gsm. II 13, VI 17, IX 7, X 5; þam, dsm. I 11, II 6, IV 32, VII 23, VIII 60, XII 21; þone, asm. I 16, IV 6, VI 7, X 8; þi, ism. VIII 27; þa, npm. I 2, III 3, IX 8; ap. VI 32; þam, dpm. VI 12; þæt, nsn. I 14, II 20, II 24, III 17, IV 4, IV 24, etc.; þæs, gsn. V 24, IX 63, IX 40; þæt, asn. II 12, V 17, VI 6, VIII 8, VIII 35, VIII 67; þam, dsn. II 22, VIII 55, X 3; þa, apn. VII 16, VIII 38, IX 18, X 29, XI 24; þara, gpn. VIII 11; seo, nsf. II 18, V 20, VI 23, VII 32, VIII 26, etc.; sio, nsf. IV 17, XII 4; þære, gsf. IV 11, XII 19; þa, asf. V 10, VIII 16, IX 42, IX 61, IX 64, XI 4.
sē þe, rel. pro., *who, he who*: nsm. II 2, II 16, II 30; þæs þe, gs. IV 2, V 26 (*since*); þone þe, as. II 6; þa þe, ap. V 12; þara þe, gp. II 31, IX 3.
se þēah (swā þēah), adv., *still, however, nevertheless*: VII 48.
searocræft, m., *skillful or clever strength*: as. I 9.
searoþoncol, adj., *shrewd, thoughtful*: ns. VIII 7.
secg, m., *man*: ns. VIII 7.
secgan, W 3, *say, tell*: inf. II 16, IV 3, V 25, IX 43; secge, 1 sg. VII 33; secgað, 3 pl. IX 5; sægde, pret. 3 sg. VII 40, IX 28; sægdon, pret. 3 pl. III 15, VI 8; saga, imp. sg. VII 46.
secge, f., *speech*: ns. VII 27.

sēl, comp. adj., *better*: sellan, apnwk. x 29.
sēlest, super. adj., *best, greatest*: selestan, gsn. IX 7.
sellan, W 1, *give*: sylle, opt. pres. 2 sg. x 28; sealdes, pret. 2 sg. IX 16.
sendan, W 1, *send*: inf. V 26; sende, pret. 3 sg. IX 20; sended, pp. V 2.
sēon, V, *see, look*: sioh, imp. sg. III 10; gesewen, pp. V 22.
seraphin, m., *seraphim*: seraphinnes, gs. XI 9.
settan, W 1, *ordain, establish, create*: sette, pret. 3 sg. VIII 23; settende, part. x 9.
sibb, f., *peace*: sibbe, gs. III 1.
sibsum, adj., *peaceful, pacific*: sibsuma, vsmwk. VIII 1.
sīd, adj., *broad, wide, great*: side, apm. I 5; sidan, apfwk. III 10, VIII 26, x 9; sidra, gpf. VII 7.
sīde, adv., *widely, extensively*: XI 17.
sigedrihten, m., *Victory Lord*: sigedrihtne, ds. V 25.
sigor, m., *victory*: sigores, gs. IV 18, VIII 30, IX 20, XI 27, XII 5.
sigorbeorht, adj., *triumphant (victory bright)*: nsm. I 10.
sinc, n., *treasure, gold*: since, is. IX 35.
singales, adv., *forever*: IX 49, XI 16.
singan, III, *sing*: singað, 3 pl. IX 9, XI 11.
sinneahtes, adv., *in perpetual night*: V 14.
sittan, V, *sit, remain*: sittað, 1 pl. II 9; sæton, pret. 3 pl. V 14.
sīð, m., *expedition, journey, time*: siðe, is. III 13; siþe, is. VI 17, IX 44.
sīðian, W 2, *journey, travel*: siðade, IX 55.
siþþan, adv., *after, afterwards*: VII 31, IX 20, IX 65, IX 72, x 28, XII 23.
snūde, adv., *quickly*: IX 23.
snyttro, f., *wisdom*: ns. VIII 26.
sōfte, adv., *calmly, patiently*: VI 17.
solima, f., *Jerusalem*: Solimae, gs. IV 21.
somod, adv., *also, together with, and*: IV 21, V 22.
sōna, adv., *immediately, soon*: I 10, VIII 20.
sorg, f., *sorrow*: sorga, gp. VII 7; sorgum, dp. IV 17.
sorgcearu, f., *care, grieving*: sorgceare, as. VII 46.
sorgian, W 2, *sorrow, grieve*: sorgende, part. npm. II 9.
sorglēas, adj., *without sorrow, carefree*: sorglease, npm. IX 72.
sōð, adj., *true*: nsm. IX 43, XI 27; soða, vsmwk. VIII 1; soþan, gsmwk. V 7.
sōð, m., *truth*: as. II 16, VII 27, VII 34.
sōðe, adv., *truly*: VII 50.

## GLOSSARY AND WORD INDEX

sōðfæder, m., *Father of Truth*: ds. IV 33.
sōðfæst, adj., *true, steadfast, righteous*: sōðfæsta, vsmwk. V 3; nsm. IX 28, X 28, I 10; soðfæste, nsnwk. XI 9; soðfæstra, gpm. III 4.
sōðlīce, adv., *truly*: IV 8, VI 8, VII 40.
spēd, f., *success, faculty, means*: as. IX 22.
spelboda, m., *messenger*: ns. IX 62.
spr&aelig;c, f., *speech, charge*: spr&aelig;ce, as. VII 20.
sprecan, V, *speak, say*: sprece, opt. 1 sg. VII 27; spricest, 2 sg. VII 16; spriceð, 3 sg. II 16; sprecað, 1 pl. II 5; sprecað, 3 pl. VII 8.
stān, m., *stone*: stanum, ip. VII 29.
standan, VI, *stand*: stondað, 3 pl. IX 48; stodon, pret. 3 pl. VIII 39.
stefn, f., *voice*: stefne, is. XI 12; stefne, ap. X 13.
strong, adj., *strong*: strengre, comp. nsm. VII 29.
sum, pro., *some, a certain*: nsm. IX 28; sume, is. IX 44.
sundbūend, mpl., *men*: np. IV 3; sundbuendum dp. VIII 8.
sundurgiefu, f., *especial gift*: sundurgiefe, ds. IV 10.
sunne, f., *sun*: sunnan, gs. V 3; sunnan, as. II 9, V 11.
sunu, m., *son*: vs. V 7; ns. V 23, VI 14, VIII 23; suna, gs. IV 24; as. VII 34, VII 42, IX 23, IX 65; sunu, ds. VII 47; sunu, vp. IV 21.
sūsl, n., *torture, torment*: suslum, dp. VI 20.
swā, adv., *so*: VI 9, VI 19, VIII 20, IX 32, etc.
swā, conj., *so, as, as if*: I 17, III 9, III 14, IV 15, IV 16, V 6, V 9, VI 3, etc.
sweart, adj., *swart, black*: swearta, nsmwk. VIII 56.
swegel, n., *heaven*: swegles, gs. V 7, VII 40, IX 7.
swegle, adv., *celestially, splendidly*: XI 16.
sweltan, III, *die*: inf. VII 28.
sweotule, adv., *clearly*: VIII 30.
swīge, f., *silence*: ns. VII 27.
swīðe, adv., *strongly, exceedingly*: VIII 7, IX 36.
swylc, pro., *such*: nsf. IX 16; asn. IV 8; swylce, asf. IV 10.
swylce, adv., *also, likewise, too*: III 11, VI 16, IX 8.
sylf, pro., *self, yourself, himself, own*: nsm. III 13, V 11, IX 45, X 9; sylfa, nsmwk. I 12, III 10, V 16, VI 14, VI 20, VII 17, VIII 23, XII 20; sylfes, gs. I 9, VIII 41; sylfre, gsf. IX 65; sylfum, dsm. V 5, VII 50; sylfne, asm. V 26; sylfra, gpm. X 15.
sylle, see sellan.
symle, adv., *always, ever*: IV 18, IV 33, V 5, V 25, X 29, XII 17; simle, III 4, IX 49, XI 16, XI 27.

## GLOSSARY AND WORD INDEX

synlust, m., *propensity to sin*: as. VIII 56.
synn, f., *sin, crime*: synnum, dp. IX 16; synna, gp. VII 17; synnum, ip. V 14, V 22.
tācn, n., *token, sign*: ns. III 5.
tealtrian, W 2, *totter, waver*: tealtrigað, 1 pl. X 24.
tēar, m., *tear*: tearas, ap. VII 9.
tempel, n., *temple*: tempel, ns. VII 43; temple, ds. VII 23.
tīd, f., *time*: tid, as. XI 29; tide, ds. IV 12; tida, gp. V 4, VIII 22.
tīr, m., *glory*: tires, gs. VIII 57; tire, is. II 12.
tīrfruma, m., Originator of Glory: tirfruman, (MS tirfruma) gs. VII 43.
tō, prep., *to, in, of, as, for*: II 13, II 15, VI 19, VIII 10, VIII 42, etc.; Idioms: tō weorce, tō mēder, tō worulde, tō cwealme, etc.: I 3, II 11, II 19, III 8, III 16, III 18, IV 17, IV 31, V 21, XI 37, XII 12; tō þæs, *so*, VIII 7; tō wīdan fēore, *forever*, VIII 17, IX 3.
tō, adv., *too, excessive*: VII 18, X 26.
torht, adj., *glorious, bright*: vsm. V 4; nsm. VIII 22; torhtes, gs. VII 43; torhtan, dsnwk. VII 23.
tornword, n., *bitter word, scornful speech*: tornworda, gp. VII 9.
tōstenced, pp. adj., *scattered, dispersed*: VIII 43.
tōweard, adj., *forward, in the future, coming*: IV 12, VI 8.
tōwiðere, prep., *against*: VII 22.
tōwrecen, pp. adj., *scattered, ruined*: towrecene, asn. VIII 45.
trēow, f., *truth, faith*: ns. IV 12.
tungol, m., *star*: tunglas, ap. V 4; tunglum, dp. VIII 22.
tȳdre, adj., *weak, infirm*: asnwk. II 12; tydran, ismwk. X 24.
þā, conj., *when*: II 14, II 17, II 29, VIII 20, X 8.
þā, adv., *then*: VII 32, IX 32, IX 52, X 4.
þǣr, conj., *where, there*: IX 33, IX 72, XII 21, XII 23.
þǣr, adv., *there*: II 26, IX 53.
þæs, conj., *so, for this reason*: VIII 28 (see tō þæs).
þæt, conj., *that, which, so that, in order that*: I 4, I 7, I 12, II 7, II 17, II 21, IV 4, IV 10, IV 27, IV 30, V 10, V 12, V 20, VI 31, VII 23, VII 30, etc.
ðætte, conj., *that, that the*: VI 14, XII 2.
þe, relative particle, *that, so that, who*: I 2, II 8, II 13, II 19, II 28, III 10, IV 19, V 18, VIII 8, VIII 11, VIII 19, VIII 26, VIII 29, VIII 38, IX 18, XII 16, etc. (also see sē þe).
þēah, conj., *although*: X 21.
þearf, f., *need, duty*: ns. I 11, VIII 42, X 26; þearfe, ds. II 5; þearfum, dp. V 9.

## GLOSSARY AND WORD INDEX

þegn, m., *thane, follower*: þegnas, np. IX 9.
þegnung, f., *service, ministration*: þegnunga, ap. X 7.
þēod, f., *men, people, nation*: þeode, ds. V 24, X 30; þeoda, gp. VIII 11.
þēoden, m., *Prince, leader*: ns. IX 58; þeodnes, gs. X 7.
þēodenstōl, m., *royal throne*: as. XI 20.
þēodland, n., *inhabited region*: as. IX 32.
þēostru, n. or f., *darkness, night*: þeostrum, dp. V 13; þystro, as. VIII 14.
þēs, dem. pro., *this*: þeos, nsf. IV 10; þisses, gsn. VIII 25; þis, asn. II 15; þisne, asm. VIII 36; þisse, dsf. IX 70; þas, asf. III 10, VIII 26, IX 55, X 9; þas, apn. II 5, IX 44.
þīn, poss. pro., *thy, thine*: nsm. XI 28, X 20; asn. I 9, VIII 29, VIII 33, VIII 41, VIII 44, VIII 53; þines, gs. VI 31, XI 32; þinre, gsf. IX 65; þinne, asm. VIII 4, VIII 24, VIII 37, IX 15, X 2, X 30; þine, asf. VIII 31; þinra, gp. VIII 42, X 14; þinum, dp. VI 33.
þing, n., *thing, matter, affair*: ap. II 8?, X 29; þinges, gs. IX 59; þinga, gp. VIII 11.
þonan, conj., *thence, whence*: VIII 56.
þonc, m., *thanks*: as. V 24, VII 46.
þonne, adv., *then, therewith, when*: I 13, VI 26, VII 28, VIII 41, IX 48, XII 7.
þringan, III, *throng, crowd*: þringað, 3 pl. XI 20.
þrīst, adj., *vigorous, bold*: þristum, dpn. IX 68.
þrīsthycgende, part. adj., *strong in mind, thinking boldly*: nsf. IX 14.
þrosm, m., *smoke, darkness*: þrosme, is. V 13.
þrymlīce, adv., *splendidly, gloriously*: IX 14.
þrym, m., *glory*: as. IV 1, IV 13, VII 41; þrim, ns. XII 8; þrymmum, dp. VIII 4, XI 11.
þrynes, f. *Trinity*: ns. XI 2.
þrȳðgesteald, n., *heaven, glorious place*: as. X 7.
þū, pro., *thou*: ns. I 2, I 4, II 1, III 9, IV 5, IV 10, etc.; þe, ds. I 3, III 3, III 7, III 14, III 16, III 19, IV 4, IV 12, etc.; þec, as. III 12, V 9, VI 31, IX 4, IX 56, X 21; þe, as. VIII 9, IX 58.
þurfan, prp., *need, have reason to*: þurfon, 1 pl. IV 11.
þurh, prep., *through, by, in*: I 9, II 21, II 27, II 32, IV 6, IV 22, V 10, V 17, VII 26, etc.
þus, adv., *thus, so*: VI 27, VII 33.
unāþrēotende, part. adj., *unwearied*: ipm. XI 11.
unbrǣce, adj., *unbreakable*: unbræcne, asm. I 6.

{ 134 }

under, prep., *under*: I 14, II 28, VIII 6, VIII 13, IX 12.
unmǣle, adj., *undefiled, spotless*: asf. IX 59.
unwemme, adj., *spotless, unsoiled*: asf. IX 26; asn. XII 3.
up, adv., *up*: X 6.
upcund, adj., *heavenly, exalted*: upcundan, ds. VIII 55.
uplīc, adj., *high, heavenly*: uplican, dsmwk. IV 32.
uppe, adv., *on high, up above*: XI 10.
upweg, m., *exalted way, path to heaven*: upwegas, ap. II 3.
ūser, poss. pro., *our*: ussa (MS usse) gpf. VIII 48; ussum, dsm. II 11, XI 21; usse, apf. X 23.
ūt, adv., *out*: IX 55.
wǣrfæst, adj., *trustworthy, faithful to promises*: XI 7.
wærgðu, f. indecl., *evil, curse, condemnation*: wærgða, ns. IV 28; wærgðo, gs. III 8.
wāfian, W 2, *wonder at, marvel*: wafiað, 2 pl. IV 19.
waldend, m., *Ruler, God*: vs. VIII 45; ns. II 29, IX 54; as. VI 34, XI 17; waldende, is. VIII 27.
wē, pro., *we*: np. II 5, II 8, II 14, IV 8, IV 11, V 16, V 24, VIII 33, VIII 34, etc.; ure, gp. X 15; usic, ap. II 13, VIII 41, VIII 59, IX 71; us, dp. & ap. II 10, IV 4, V 10, V 21, V 26, VI 6, VI 21, VI 27, VI 29, VI 30, etc.
weall, m., *wall*: as. I 11; wealle, ds. I 11; weallas, ap. I 5.
wealldor, n., *gate*: ns. IX 54.
weallstān, m., *corner stone*: ns. I 2.
weard, m., *guardian, ruler*: ns. VI 5, VIII 9, VIII 30.
weardian, W 2, *protect, guard*: weardiað (MS wearð) 3 pl. XI 19.
wel, adv., *rightly, well*: I 3.
wēn, f., *opinion, supposition*: wene, ds. VII 49.
wēnan, W 1, *expect, hope for, think*: inf. IV 11; wenað, 1 pl. II 9; wende, pret. 3 sg. IX 36.
weorc, n., *work, deed*: ns. II 4; as. I 9; weorce, ds. I 3, I 11.
weorc, m., *affliction, pain*: weorcum, dp. III 8.
weorod, n., *people, men, a group, multitude*: weoroda, gp. VI 32, VIII 16, IX 73, XI 30, XII 13; weorodum, dp. V 17.
weorðan, III, *become, be*: weorþeð, 3 sg. III 6; wearð, pret. 3 sg. II 21, II 26, IV 14, VII 37; weorðe, opt. 3 sg. II 11; weorðen, opt. 3 pl. VIII 19; geworden, pp. II 20.
weorðian, W 2, *worship, honor*: inf. XI 17; weorðige, opt. 3 sg. XII 18; weorðien, opt. 3 pl. VI 31.
weorðlīc, adj., *worthy, exalted*: weorðlicu, nsf. IV 13.
weorðmynd, f., *honor, praise*: weorðmynda, gp. XI 1.

## GLOSSARY AND WORD INDEX

wer, m., *man*: weres, gs. II 20, XII 4; wera, gp. XII 1; werum, dp. IV 31.

wērig, adj., *weary, dejected, damned*: wergan, asmwk. I 16; wergan, npm. X 16; wergum, dp. VI 22, VIII 51.

wesan, anom., see bēon.

wīd, adj., *wide, long*: widan, asmwk. XII 24; widan, dsmwk. VIII 17, IX 3 (see tō).

wīde, adv., *widely*: VII 22, VIII 45, XI 17, XI 30.

wīdeferh, adv., *lifelong, for a long time, forever*: VI 34.

wīf, n., *woman, wife*: wifes, gs. II 23; wifa, gp. IV 1; wifum, dp. IV 31.

wīgend, m., *warrior, men*: wigendra, gp. XI 32.

wiht, n., *whit, anything*: (MS niht) as. XII 4.

willa, m., *will, purpose*: willan, as. X 30.

willan, anom., *wish, will*: wile, 3 sg. IX 45; willað, 3 pl. II 32; wolde, pret. 3 sg. V 26, VI 14; wille, opt. 2 sg. VIII 61.

wilsīþ, n., *desired journey*: wilsiþes, gs. II 4.

wīse, f., *shoot, sprout*: wisna, gp. II 26.

wīse, f., *thing, matter*: wisan, as. VIII 16, IX 42.

wīsfæst, adj., *wise, sagacious*: nsm. IX 32; wisfæste, npm. III 15.

witan, prp., *know*: inf. XI 7.

wīte, n., *pain, torture*: wites, gs. VIII 51.

wītedōm, m., *prophecy*: as. VII 49.

wīteþēow, m., *tormented slave*: witeþeowum, dp. VI 22.

wītga, m., *prophet, wise man*: witga, ns. IX 32; witgan, np. III 15; witgena, gp. II 29.

witig, adj., *wise, intelligent*: nsm. VIII 13.

wið, prep., *with, against, towards*: I 11, X 21.

wiðweorpan, III, *reject, throw away*: wiðwurpon, pret. 3 pl. I 3.

wlātian, W 2, *gaze, look*: wlatade, pret. 3 sg. IX 53.

wlītan, I, *see, view*: wlat, pret. 3 sg. IX 32.

wlitig, adj., *beautiful*: wlitige, nsf. XI 1, wlitigan, gsmwk. II 4.

wolcen, m., *sky, heaven*: wolcnum, dp. VIII 13.

womm, m., *spot, stain, sin*: wommes, gs. III 5; womma, gp. VII 16, VII 25.

wone, indec. adj., *lacking, wanting*: VIII 57.

wōp, m., *tears, weeping*: wope, ds. VI 22.

word, n., *word*: as. IX 42; ap. II 5, V 17, VII 16, XI 24; word*a* (MS worde) gp. VII 6; wordum, dp. III 15, IX 68, XII 14.

worldcund, adj., *earthly, mundane*: nsm. VII 49: world*c*undra (MS worlcundra) gp. IX 11.

worn, m., *much, a great deal*: as. VII 6.

{ 136 }

## GLOSSARY AND WORD INDEX

woruld, f., *world*: worulde, gs. VIII 4; worlde, ds. II 23; tō wor(u)lde, *forever*: I 8, IV 31.
wōðbora, n., *wise man, prophet*: ns. IX 28.
wōðsong, m., *song, speech-song, prophecy*: ns. II 29.
wræclīc, adj., *strange, marvelous*: ns. XII 1.
wræcmæcg, m., *wretch, evil spirit*: wræcmæcgas, np. X 16.
wrāþ, adj. as noun, *hostile, angry, inimical*: wraþum, dpm. I 16, VII 22.
wrecca, m., *wretch, exile*: wreccan, ds. VIII 51.
wrixl, f., *change, alteration*: ns. XII 1.
wuldor, n., *glory*: wuldres, gs. I 8, IV 1, IV 13, VI 29, VI 31, XI 32; wuldre, ds. II 13, III 8, V 7, IX 73; wuldrum, dp. III 5.
wuldorcyning, m., *King of Glory*: as. VI 32.
wuldorweorud, n., *heavenly host*: wuldorweorudes, gs. IX 11.
wuldrian, W 2, *glorify*: wuldriað, 3 pl. XI 24.
wulf, m., *wolf*: ns. VIII 43.
wundrian, W 2, *admire, wonder at*: wundrien, opt. 3 pl. I 8.
wundrung, f., *wondering, puzzlement*: nsf. IV 19.
wundurclomm, n., *wondrous band, fetter*: wundurclommum, dp. IX 36.
wunian, W 2, *dwell*: inf. IV 33; wunigan, IX 73; wunast, 2 sg. VI 34; wunað, 3 sg. XI 28, XII 24; wunade, pret. 3 sg. IV 13.
wynn, f., *joy*: vs. IV 1; wynne, ds. XII 22.
wyrcan, W 1, *make, create*: worhtes, pret. 2 sg. VIII 27.
wyrd, f., *event, happening*: wyrde, gs. IV 11.
wyrhta, m., *worker, builder*: wyrhtan, np. I 2.
wyrp, m., *alleviation, improvement*: wyrpe, ds. III 18.
wyrðe, adj., *worthy, deserving*: apm. II 13.
ymb, prep., *on, around*: III 12, XI 20.
yrmðu, see ermðu.
ȳwan, W 1, *show, manifest*: ywe, imp. sg. VIII 32.

The Advent (*Anglo-Saxon lyrics*) The Advent lyrics of the Exeter book. Edited, with introd. and notes, by Jackson J. Campbell. Princeton, N.J., Princeton University Press, 1959. x, 137 p. 24 cm. Text in Anglo-Saxon and English. Erroneously ascribed to Cynewulf as pt. 1 of his poem The Christ. Bibliographical references included in "Notes" (p. 81-101) Bibliography: p. 105-107. 1. Campbell, Jackson Justice, 1920- ed. and tr. II. Title. PR1519.A3 1959 (829.1082) 59-5592 Library of Congress.

GPSR Authorized Representative: Easy Access System Europe - Mustamäe tee 50, 10621 Tallinn, Estonia, gpsr.requests@easproject.com

www.ingramcontent.com/pod-product-compliance
Lightning Source LLC
Chambersburg PA
CBHW051527230426
43668CB00012B/1771